ENDORSEMENTS

What unfolds in this book is the testimony o
to realize that he was born into a battlefield,
supernatural is not an abstract idea for Tony—it is the backdrop of his life, his ministry, and his assignment.

Tony doesn't approach this mission as a theorist—he writes as a man who has *seen, wrestled,* and *walked through* the collision of two worlds to inherit his calling. His story is not just compelling; it's a wake-up call for us all.

But be warned, there is a weight to this message—a reality that what has been handed down must be carried forward. Tony writes with the conviction of someone who understands that the war is real, the enemy is active, and the Church can no longer afford to remain asleep.

In these pages, Tony exposes what many have experienced, but few have the courage to articulate: we are living in a world where the veil is thin, the battle is real, and the stakes are eternal.

If you've ever sensed that there is more going on behind the scenes than what meets the eye, this book will both confirm it and challenge you to take your own place in the fight.

Vicki Joy Anderson
Author of *From Eden to A.I.*

We are all on a journey in the Kingdom, and here, my good friend Tony Merkel pulls back the veil on the war raging around us. The red pill turns out to be the blood of Jesus in this exclusive confession from the confessional himself.

I love Tony, know him personally, and have been looking forward to this one. He doesn't just tell stories about the unseen realm; he exposes it. UFOs, dogman, cryptids, the things that go bump in the night—Tony shows you the spiritual intelligence operating behind all of it, and the Kingdom that stands against it.

Get yourself ready to consider the supernatural without stained glass and absent of hymn books. In the midst of monsters, Tony points to the King of all creatures, holy and fallen. Tony is proof that if you are a seeker, you will be a finder.

Troy Brewer
Senior Pastor, OpenDoor Church
Author of 16 books
Rescuer of over 12,000 children worldwide

Tony Merkel has done something most people in the church are afraid to attempt. He walked straight into the places Christians pretend don't exist, shone a light, and brought back documented intelligence from the front lines of a war that is very real and very active.

This isn't fringe content dressed up in spiritual language. *The Confessionals: Exposing Warring Kingdoms* is a serious, biblically grounded reckoning with UFOs, cryptids, interdimensional entities, and the coordinated deception coming for the church. Tony doesn't chase sensationalism. He follows the evidence, tests it against Scripture, and arrives at a conclusion that should wake up every pastor, every believer, and every person willing to ask honest questions about what is actually happening around us.

What sets this book apart is Tony's discernment. He doesn't lead you into the mystery and leave you there. He equips you to stand. The testimony threads woven through these chapters aren't curiosities; they're a map. And Tony reads that map with clarity, courage, and a pastoral urgency that reflects someone who has personally paid a price for the message he carries.

If you've been sitting on the fence about how serious this supernatural war is, this book will take the fence out from under you. Read it, share it with your pastor, and get your house built on something solid before the storm arrives.

Shaun Tabatt
Publisher, Destiny Image
Author of *Accessing the Realms of Heaven*

Over the past few years, my friend Tony Merkel has built a highly successful channel, *The Confessionals*, that examines shocking topics—not without controversy, but certainly driven by an obsession to know the truth. He is deeply informed, as any listener would recognize, as he poses questions and leads conversations that elicit answers. His material and depth of insight led him down a path he might not have seen coming. An evolution began in Tony's life, not only in the space he has developed but also in a higher, much greater significance.

Early in my time observing him, the journey was beginning. Tony discovered that he was to begin glorifying the Name of Jesus and fully embrace the call of God on his life, which is to advance the Kingdom of God. Tony's curiosity and desire to understand unexplained happenings and phenomena led him to a place of great significance, the place where God begins to call a man into higher service. This has not come without some of the hardest challenges a man can face. Yet, at each point, I have seen him rise to the occasion, seeking the Lord with a deep desire to walk out his calling.

This book is a snapshot of Tony's journey, from his youth to the startling experiences he has encountered along the way, leading to the Confessionals channel and beyond.

What Tony has created with this book is an insightful document, written from a first-hand insider's perspective, into the spiritual battles being waged today. Tony has boldly gone where the Church has often refused to look, standing on the "Frontier" to bear witness to the shocking truth: the thin veil between our world and the unseen realm is rapidly tearing open.

Through his journey from skeptic to "Guardian of the Frontier", Tony dismantles the comfortable lie that the supernatural is not merely historical or mythological. He provides chilling, undeniable evidence that the so-called cryptids, UFOs, and paranormal phenomena are not aliens or undiscovered animals, but are, as he describes them, ancient "principalities and powers" that Paul warned us about in Ephesians 6:12.

The testimonies within *The Confessionals: Exposing Warring Kingdoms* are gripping and insightful to comprehend a fast-rising end-times deception: from a classified military mission encountering Enochian—the language of fallen angels—on a downed aircraft, to physical claw marks left by a dogman who attacked a man in a dream state. This book, through its off-the-beaten-path narrative, proves that the war is raging and that the enemy is operating across dimensional boundaries to sow fear and confusion.

If you know something is wrong with the world, if you sense the rising darkness, or if you simply need to understand the true nature of the battle, you're already in. *The Confessionals: Exposing Warring*

Kingdoms is both a prophetic warning and a powerful call to repentance, to spiritual authority, and to full surrender to Jesus Christ. The protection and power of God are real, but you have the opportunity to know the enemy's script and stand your ground.

Keep your eye on Tony Merkel because the best is yet to come!

Joseph Z
Author, Broadcaster, Prophetic Voice
JosephZ.com

Tony Merkel has stepped into a conversation that many in the church have been hesitant to address, and he does it with boldness, discernment, and a strong biblical perspective. *The Confessionals: Exposing Warring Kingdoms* takes readers into some of the most mysterious and controversial topics of our time while continually pointing back to the reality of spiritual warfare and the authority of Jesus Christ.

In a generation filled with confusion, deception, fear, and endless speculation, this book challenges believers to stay spiritually awake, grounded in Scripture, and led by the Holy Spirit instead of hype or sensationalism. Whether discussing UFOs, cryptids, or unseen spiritual realities, Tony consistently brings the conversation back to the battle between darkness and light and the need for discernment in this hour.

I believe this is a timely and important work that will encourage many believers to deepen their understanding of spiritual warfare, strengthen their faith, and keep their focus on Jesus Christ and the truth of God's Word.

Pastor Todd Coconato

Tony Merkel did not write a paranormal book. He wrote a field report from a spiritual war that most people do not know they are standing in the middle of. Every story in this book, from dogmen to portal rituals to prophetic dreams, with 98 percent accuracy, lands in the same place: the name of Jesus is the only name that carries authority over all of it. Tony lives this, and it shows on every page.

There are people who talk about the supernatural, and there are people who have been marked by it. This book takes you inside the experiences that forged both *The Confessionals* and the man behind it, building an argument that is deeply personal and theologically serious. Tony is not asking you to believe in the paranormal. He is asking you to recognize that the paranormal, the biblical, and the battle for your soul are the same conversation.

Luke Rogers
Host, *Blurry Creatures*

The Confessionals: Exposing Warring Kingdoms kicks the door open on the conversation most churches got too polished to have. Tony Merkel walks you straight into the smoke with a flashlight and brings you out the other side with biblical clarity, courage, and the head of a Nephilim.

Ignorance isn't bliss. People perish for a lack of knowledge.

Get equipped. Read this book.

Darren Stott
Pastor, Author, Real-Life Ghostbuster

Tony Merkel has carried a rare assignment for this generation, and *The Confessionals: Exposing Warring Kingdoms* proves it throughout every chapter. This is more than a collection of strange encounters. Tony takes the reader into the places most people avoid, where UFOs, cryptids, dreams, portals, demonic activity, and spiritual warfare all begin to point to a much larger conflict.

What I appreciate about Tony is that he does not treat the supernatural like entertainment. He handles it like a watchman. He investigates, listens, asks hard questions, and then he brings the whole conversation back to the authority of Jesus Christ. That matters. In a generation being conditioned to accept every strange sign and wonder at face value, the Church needs voices who can discern the difference between mystery and deception.

This book will challenge the skeptic, strengthen the believer, and wake up anyone willing to admit that the unseen war is real. Tony writes with honesty, courage, and deep conviction. I am honored to call him my friend, and I highly recommend this powerful and timely book.

Pastor Larry Ragland
Solid Rock Church, Birmingham, Alabama
Host of *The Big Picture Podcast*
Author of *The Final Flood and I See Greatness In You*

I have known Tony Merkel for several years, not only as the voice behind *The Confessionals,* but as a trusted and close friend. Tony is genuine, honest, a devoted family man, and a servant of God. Some of what he lays out in this book may seem inconceivable, especially in a modern church culture that has often lost its awareness of the supernatural realm. Yet, I have watched Tony walk through much of this journey personally. I know many of the behind-the-scenes details, and more importantly, I know the man behind the stories. I also know the supernatural is not fringe—it is the deeper reality.

Tony's purpose is not sensationalism. His desire is to expose the supernatural battle hidden just behind the veil, a veil that often conceals a sinister agenda, and to point readers to Jesus Christ as the Victor, Savior, and only sure hope in this spiritual war.

This book is an easy, powerful, and fast-paced read. You will learn from it, be challenged by it, and your eyes may be opened to supernatural deceptions that many are falling prey to.

I wholeheartedly endorse this book—partly because I already know many of the stories, but mostly because I trust Tony Merkel. I believe he has written this with courage, conviction, and a sincere desire to lead people to the truth found in Jesus Christ.

Pastor Jerry R. Laudermilk

THE CONFESSIONALS

EXPOSING WARRING KINGDOMS

THE CONFESSIONALS

EXPOSING WARRING KINGDOMS

THE HIDDEN TRUTH BEHIND
UFOS, CRYPTIDS, AND
SPIRITUAL WARFARE

TONY MERKEL

DESTINY IMAGE® PUBLISHERS, INC.
P.O. Box 310, Shippensburg, PA 17257-0310
"Publishing cutting-edge prophetic resources to supernaturally empower the body of Christ"

This book and all other Destiny Image and Destiny Image Fiction books are available at Christian bookstores and distributors worldwide.

For more information on foreign distributors, call 717-532-3040.
Reach us on the Internet: www.destinyimage.com.

ISBN 13 TP: 979-8-8815-0813-5
ISBN 13 eBook: 979-8-8815-0814-2

For Worldwide Distribution, Printed in the U.S.A.
1 2 3 4 5 6 7 8 / 30 29 28 27 26

Contents

Foreword

The supernatural world is real and surrounds us and sometimes manifests to people like you and me.

Tony Merkel is on the front lines of spiritual warfare. He is committed to revealing to what I would call *a sleeping Church* the stark reality of the *invisible war* that is raging all around us.

The book opens up when Tony is just a boy, and when he goes into the woods in Kutztown, Pennsylvania, he senses there is more than what meets his eyes—he senses the supernatural world that indeed surrounds us. That sense is a gift that not many people possess.

This is the beginning of a journey that plunged Tony into the reality of the demonic world and what is called out by Paul the Apostle: "*For we wrestle not against flesh and blood, but against principalities, against powers, against the rulers of the darkness of this world, against spiritual wickedness in high places*" (Ephesians 6:12).

Then there is the passing of Tony's spiritual father, or I should say his grandfather literally.

I will tell you a connection I have with Tony that blew me away. I grew up in Berwyn, Pennsylvania, and there is a town called Newtown Square which is only a few minutes away.

When I was still a teenager, I found myself with a buddy outside a tent on a mid-summer's night. There was a preacher talking about Jesus. I made fun of him, as at that time I was unsaved. I told Tony about this, and he and I believe I saw his grandfather preaching! What an amazing connection. Were seeds planted that night? Absolutely!

So, with Tony's grandfather's passing, his spiritual covering gone, it is now up to Tony to forge his own path forward, and as you will see, with the help of the Spirit of the Living God, this is exactly what happens.

The road forward is not an easy one, and it is fraught with the pushback from the enemy of our souls. Once again, Tony is experiencing, firsthand, the machinations of the Dragon who comes only to rob, kill, and destroy—and without giving away the chapter that deals with this, let me say Tony came face to face with evil and those who embrace it.

The Lord spoke to Tony, telling him to start a podcast, and as most of you know, Tony created *The Confessionals* podcast that reaches thousands of people on a weekly basis.It is here where Tony comes into his anointing as he explores all things supernatural, or to be more succinct, *things you'll never hear in most churches!*

Tony embraces all things supernatural, and like my battle-buddy author and demonologist Russ Dizdar, he's not afraid to confront the darkness head-on. As you will see, no subject is off limits!

We are, in fact, in the midst of two *warring kingdoms*—but we know who will win in the end!

In these troublesome times that we find ourselves living in, this book shines a light on the burgeoning dark deception that is all around us.

Buckle up. Get prayed up and read this book slowly. Ask the Holy Spirit to reveal the deeper things that Tony covers. And remember, we have not been given a spirit of fear, but of love, power, and a sound mind.

Dr. L.A. Marzulli
Author/Filmmaker

1
The Veil Was Always Thin

...the god of this world has blinded the minds of the unbelievers, to keep them from seeing the light of the gospel of the glory of Christ, who is the image of God.

—2 Corinthians 4:4 ESV

Life is full of the supernatural and experiences with it. The more you learn, the more you see it. But most of us are trained from childhood not to see it, not to talk about it, not to believe it's there. We're told to grow up, be rational, trust only what science can measure. But what if the problem isn't that we see too much, but that we've been blinded to what's actually there?

When I was a kid, I grew up in rural Pennsylvania. Kutztown, Pennsylvania, to be exact. I was a trailer-park kid growing up in Highland Estates trailer park, which is one of the largest trailer parks I have ever seen. Hundreds of trailers with families that have thousands of issues. It was a very rough way to spend my childhood. Lots of fights, alcohol, tobacco, and drug use among the youth of the neighborhood. I partook in all of the above except the drugs. Not that I didn't want to, but rather I was afraid of my father. I knew I could hide the alcohol and tobacco smells because he smoked cigars at the time himself. But hiding a high from him would be more challenging, and if he caught me high, well, I don't know if I would be writing this book today.

I had very few friends in this neighborhood as the social structure was very complex, and I often found myself at the bottom of the proverbial totem pole of social hierarchy. Of the friends I did have, we would go down into the woods on hot summer days to get lost in our imaginations and steer clear of parents and bullies. We would build complex tree houses, mostly made of other people's property that we would find "lying around" and consider free for the taking.

We would find pulleys and make harnesses to sit in so we could pull ourselves up to the tree house platforms. I stopped using those the day I slipped with the rope and fell to the ground. I landed on my feet on top of a few wooden boards we had lying around. My initial thought was that I was pretty lucky to land on my feet and not get hurt, but as I lifted my foot to move, I realized I had landed on a nail that had gone right through my sneaker and into my foot. As I pulled my shoe off to see the damage, I immediately faced a red, blood-dripping sock, and that was all it took for me to never go back up in that tree house again.

While down in the woods, we would collect large rocks and build a wall in the creek bed. We would stack the rocks until they were protruding out of the water, creating a dam that we were sure proud of. Then we "found" a tarp that clearly none of the neighbors were using and put that down on top of the rocks. It created a nice swimming hole for us to cool off in the summer without having to go to the neighborhood swimming pool that had all the troublemakers. You can only go through a handful of almost drownings by the hands of bullies before you pull the plug and choose to be hot rather than dead.

PASSING THROUGH A THRESHOLD

Being in the woods became a sanctuary of sorts for me. I would go down there alone to get away when other friends were unable to come outside to run wild with me. I often found myself wondering about what lurks in the shadows while in those woods. There was a narrow opening when I first stepped toward the woods to enter. Often, when I would go alone, I would feel like I was passing through a threshold of some kind as I stepped into this magical forest. Looking back on it now, I would call it a portal. A portal to another world.

What I didn't realize at the time was how close that idea was to what Scripture actually says. Jacob had his moment in the wilderness when he woke from a dream of angels ascending and descending a ladder, and he said, *"...Surely the Lord is in this place, and I did not know it. ...This is none other than the house of God, and this is the gate of heaven"* (Genesis 28:16-17 ESV). That's what the woods felt like to me—a thin place, a threshold. I couldn't explain it as a kid, but I knew when I stepped through, I wasn't just in trees and dirt. I was in a place where the veil felt thinner.

The biblical writers understood this concept deeply. They knew there were places where the boundary between our world and the unseen realm became permeable. Mount Sinai wrapped in supernatural fire (Exodus 19:18). The Jordan River where the heavens tore open (Matthew 3:16). Elisha's servant suddenly saw the hills full of horses and chariots of fire (2 Kings 6:17). These weren't just geographical locations—they were intersection points between Heaven and earth.

A world that existed within ours. But it was a secret world. A world that adults didn't explore.

Not that they couldn't, but something happens to adults, and they stop dreaming about life. They lose the wonder of the unknown. That was a reality I understood from a young age. Jesus said something about this: *"Truly, I say to you, unless you turn and become like children, you will never enter the kingdom of heaven"* (Matthew 18:3 ESV). There's something about child-like awareness that sees what cynical adult eyes miss. I didn't want that to happen to me, but figured the odds were stacked against me since all the adults I knew lived this life full of gray.

A TIMELESS ENVIRONMENT

When I stepped into those woods through the portal, I entered a timeless environment. The outside world carried on, but where I was going, time didn't exist. It was the escape. The escape that I couldn't help but notice was that, though I was alone and safe, I was being watched and observed. It left me wondering if the legendary Bigfoot could truly be real, and was he in these woods with me? Watching me? Waiting for the right moment to reveal himself?

Though in the moment I would grow fearful, the world outside those woods seemed much scarier most of the time. So I would press on. Deeper into the shadows of the canopy. Further into my imagination.

My friends and I would often sit around musing on the idea of going to Scotland and hunting down the Loch Ness

Monster. We had seen a drawing of it in a book along with personal encounter stories that we borrowed from the library, and so we knew it had to be true! We couldn't fathom the idea that this creature still existed today, and no one tried to catch it. We were determined to solve that mystery when we became adults. Ironically enough, though all our lives went different directions, mine found its way back to the idea of hunting monsters that shouldn't exist. And the friends I hunt them with? They're a whole new crew of believers in the unbelievable. (More on that later.)

Though I didn't consider it then as a child, all the things I was interested in, like cryptids and mysteries of the universe, pointed me back to the reality of our supernatural existence. It has been the underlying driving theme of my life. No matter what stage of life I find myself in, high school, focusing on basketball, to college, driving a truck, or building a media company, it always comes back to my deep interest in the supernatural realm.

My mom is like this, too, and though she never explicitly expressed it, I knew I had a companion in "wanting to believe" in the extraordinary. I don't hold a lot of good memories from my childhood, though I believe they are there; my brain seems to have blocked them out, or they have simply been lost in time. I think that a person can only hold so much information in their brain before they need to discard some to make room for new information. That might be something my brain has done several times over the years.

I do remember one particular night in the trailer park. My dad was and still is a tractor-trailer driver. If anyone is familiar with the industry, they can attest that it involves a lot of unpredictable hours. You get a start time, but telling your loved ones when you will be home is not as easy as them telling you when you need to start every day. That night, Dad was working late. I do not recall when this particular story occurred. I don't remember how old I was, but I was still in the trailer park, so it was before 9th grade when we moved.

I must have been taking my dog out to use the yard. I remember I would often look to my right, deep into the back of this narrow yard between our trailer and the next. It would be pitch black beyond a tree in the center of our backyard. I would pray that my dog was enough to defend me from whatever was inevitably hiding back there, waiting to pounce on me.

This particular night, I mustered up enough courage or curiosity to look around a little while I scolded my dog for taking too long to find his spot to do his business. I looked to my left, where the empty car cement pad sat for my dad's car. Since Dad's car wasn't there, I had a clear view of the trailers across the road. Beyond those trailers was a field where we would steal the farmer's hay bales to make forts. He caught us a few times and would yell from his pickup truck at us. We would just take off and hope he didn't know where we actually lived. Funny enough, he stopped yelling at us when we stopped taking the bales of hay. As long as we built our forts in his field, he seemed not to care as much. Looking back as an adult now, I can see the sensitive nature of wanting to let kids be kids as long as possible, just as long as they aren't hurting anything.

MOVEMENT IN THE DARKNESS

As I peered into the dark field behind the trailers, imagining that whatever was in the back of my yard had a companion in that field and they were surrounding me, something caught my attention. Not in the field, but rather in the sky. It was a bright light illuminating the darkness of the sky, and it was moving. Now, I'm already in daydream mode, and one can assume I was seeing a plane in the sky. Though we were deep in the country and these lights were not common, it's still a reasonable thing to consider. But this light was lower than I would consider a plane to be flying with no airport remotely close to where we lived. We would need to drive to the Lehigh Valley Airport for any flight, which was a good hour away from where we lived. In my confusion about what I was looking at, it changed direction.

That is when I knew I needed my mother.

I dragged the dog back in the house in a panic and yelled for my mom to come outside to look at what I was seeing. I needed her to see it. To tell me that it's just a plane. But I needed her to see it, so I wouldn't be left wondering what it was and chalking it up to just something I had blown out of proportion.

I rushed through the front door into the living room and yelled for my mom to come outside with me because "there's a UFO outside," and she needed to come see it. To her credit and my surprise, she actually promptly got up out of her chair in the kitchen and ran out the door with me. As I turned to go out the door, I had every hope that the light was still moving low across the sky, but fully expecting it to be gone, and left being the overreactive kid. As I peeled across our porch and launched myself down the steps, I looked out across the field, and it's still there, and it's closer than it was before.

I remember it was now going left, then right, but it was no longer a single light. It had become four lights. One light on the left and one light on the right, perfectly parallel and moving in sync with one another. There were two more lights, one above the parallel light line the other two lights made, as well as one below that parallel line. These two lights were offset, though, and not in a straight up-and-down line. As these four lights moved across the field, perfectly spaced and not independently moving, it gave me the sense that they were connected to an object. As I anxiously watched, the lights approached the woods that I roamed daily during the summertime.

Suddenly, the magical forest I roamed just became even more magical as these sets of lights closed in on my escape from reality. The things I only imagined were now invading the place that was to be for pretend and escape. Suddenly, the two worlds were colliding before my eyes. As this set of lights approached the tree line, a bright white light shot down on a 45-degree angle from the four lights and lit up the tree line.

By now, my mom was standing outside with me, watching this whole interaction unfold right before our eyes. I don't recall what we were saying to each other, but I remember what happened next. The light beam was cut off, and the set of four lights shifted direction again, starting to move toward us at a fairly steady speed.

RUNNING TOWARD THE LIGHTS

Looking back on this, my reaction was not what you might think it would be. I was a kid seeing lights in the sky doing things that were foreign to him, and all the while, at a time of day that I was already considering the monsters in the dark. I should have run inside our trailer with my mom and locked the door, hoping the little green men wouldn't come down and visit us.

Instead, my mom and I ran from our yard, across our cement car pad, toward the lights as they came toward us. As we were set to have a one-on-one meeting with these lights over our road, the lights changed back to one solid light and shifted direction to go up the road, completely silent. There were no propulsion sounds coming from this light. I found myself alone, running up the road after a light in the sky and yelling for my mom to come, though she had no intention of running up the hill of the road with me.

I was captivated by the moment. I didn't want it to end. I had so many questions that I could not formulate one into words. I had just seen something so outside the realm of normal that I lacked understanding of how even to comprehend what we had just witnessed.

Looking back, my actions remind me of a scene from the movie *Independence Day* with Will Smith, where the woman obsessed with UFOs went up on the roof of a building where the giant UFO was hovering, joining in on a party of hippie people who wanted to be abducted by the UFO. I was that enamored, or maybe even hypnotized, by it. Nothing else mattered. My usual fears were gone, and all I wanted was to be locked in time with this thing, where time stood still, so I could just take my time to soak it up. To understand it. To let my paradigm shift completely.

But as I ran, the light glided faster, completely silent, out of sight. I walked back down the road to our trailer in the dark, suddenly not fearing what was lurking over my shoulder because whatever I had just experienced was far more real in the moment than any shadow of my imagination.

Later that night, both my mom and I told Dad when he got home. He asked a few questions but ultimately didn't have much to say because he didn't experience it with us. But that night was a precursor to the wacky, wild ride my life would become as I progressed in my understanding that reality is not what we have always been told it is.

ANCIENT WARNINGS

Years later, I would learn that what I saw wasn't unique. Throughout Scripture, there are warnings about deception in the last days. Jesus Himself warned that there will be *"great signs and wonders, so as to lead astray, if possible, even the elect"* (Matthew 24:24 ESV). Paul wrote about satan disguising himself as an *"angel of light"* (2 Corinthians 11:14 ESV). The prophet Joel spoke of *"wonders in the heavens and on the earth"* before the day of the Lord (Joel 2:30 ESV). What if these lights in the sky—these things we call UFOs—aren't what they appear to be? What if they're part of something ancient, something that's been deceiving humanity since the Garden?

The Western church has done a really good job of stripping the supernatural out of the Bible and our sermons. But the Bible itself doesn't shy away from the supernatural; it leans into it. Paul reminded the Corinthians that *"the kingdom of God is not a matter of talk but of power"* (1 Corinthians 4:20 NIV). Hebrews says, *"Jesus Christ is the same yesterday and today and forever"* (Hebrews 13:8 NIV). Because God split seas, sent fire from Heaven, and gave fishermen the power to heal in the book of Acts, why would we assume He stopped? God's Word, the Bible, doesn't give us permission to tame God into something manageable. It tells us to expect His Spirit to move in ways that shake our categories. Jesus Himself was God in human form, delivered to us by way of a virgin. Fire had fallen from

Heaven, seas split, warriors displayed supernatural strength, and fishermen healed people through the power of God.

However, that was all "then" and is no longer expected today—at least that's what we're taught. On the opposite side is the secular worldview, which needs to have a scientific explanation for everything. If science can't explain it, then it's not supernatural; it's just something science can't explain just yet. The magic of today will be the science of tomorrow, they say.

But what if the world is far more supernatural than we can even comprehend? What if the signs and wonders we read about in the Bible are just the tip of the iceberg, and what we will experience in our lifetime will make you feel like you've stumbled across a lost chapter of an Old Testament book because it feels that biblically supernatural?

As I quickly approach my 40th birthday, I want to reflect on what I have learned so far regarding the supernatural realm and how God has strategically guided me to this point, navigating life scenarios that many people can't imagine are real, but I assure you, they are.

OUR SUPERNATURAL WORLD

We are supernatural beings living in a supernatural world, and we have always been living in a supernatural war that is all about you. That's not me being dramatic, that's Ephesians 6:12 (KJV): *"For we wrestle not against flesh and blood, but against principalities, against powers, against the rulers of the darkness of this world, against spiritual wickedness in high places."* Daniel chapter 10 gives us the curtain pulled back—angels delayed in battle for 21 days while Daniel prayed, heavenly warfare raging in real time over the prince of Persia. From the beginning to the end of Scripture, it's clear you were born into a battlefield. Whether you believe in it or not, you are already in it.

This war is a desperate attempt to separate you from God forever. The enemy knows his time is short (Revelation 12:12), and he's pulling out all the stops. The deception is ramping up. The veil is thinning. What was hidden is being revealed. And you need to know which side you're on before it's too late.

I hope that as you read this book, you will come to a deeper understanding that the supernatural realm is real, active, and you need to live your life accordingly. If you know Christ as your Savior, I pray that this book helps deepen your understanding of who He is and how His creation operates.

If you don't care to know Christ as your Savior, please continue to read because I'm going to share one heck of a story that will, at the very least, activate your imagination. But who knows, when it's all said and done, you might feel the need to reconsider some of your positions if you conclude that what I am saying is true.

The encounter with those lights in the Pennsylvania sky was only the beginning. It was a spark that hinted at a larger reality, one that refused to let me settle for the ordinary explanations people cling to. From that night on, I knew there was more—something layered beneath the surface of the world I was told was normal.

But as much as the supernatural was breaking in from the outside, there was also a story unfolding inside my own family line. A story that carried the weight of inheritance, protection, and calling. The prophet Joel had written, *"And it shall come to pass afterward, that I will pour out my Spirit on all flesh;*

your sons and your daughters shall prophesy, your old men shall dream dreams, and your young men shall see visions" (Joel 2:28 ESV). I didn't know it yet, but I was part of a spiritual lineage that went back generations.

If the woods behind my trailer park taught me about wonder, and the UFO in the sky introduced me to mystery, then my grandfather's life would show me what it looked like when the supernatural walked right into the middle of an ordinary man's life. His hands, his prayers, his mantle—all of it would shape the foundation I didn't even know I was standing on.

And so, before I could understand the battles I would fight, I had to understand the man who showed me what it meant to be a Guardian of the Frontier.

2
Guardian of the Frontier

When they had crossed, Elijah said to Elisha, "Tell me, what can I do for you before I am taken from you?" "Let me inherit a double portion of your spirit," Elisha replied.

—2 Kings 2:9 NIV

"It was these two hands," my grandfather whispered, "that went on somebody's head and prayed, and that person walked away healed. And once that happens, you're a different person."

That was one of the last things he ever said to me, his frail body bent over itself in a hospital bed, his voice barely more than breath. But he wasn't bragging. He wasn't trying to make himself sound holy. He was stating a fact. If my grandfather said something happened, you could take it to the bank. He was one of the very few people in my life who had never let me down.

And here's the thing, I wasn't even his blood relative.

My mother had me just after her eighteenth birthday. My biological father was younger than she was, and nowhere near ready to be a dad. So from the beginning, I was raised by my mom, my grandmother, and eventually by the man who would become my dad, Brian. And Brian's father was Jack Walter Merkel. The man who became my grandfather. These men stepped into my life when they didn't have to and claimed me as their own.

Looking back now, I can see God's fingerprints all over that situation. The prophet Malachi wrote about God turning *"the heart of fathers to the children"* (Malachi 4:6 KJV), and that's exactly what happened. Men who had no biological obligation to me became the fathers I needed. But at the time, it was just my life, and it didn't feel divine or extraordinary.

My mom began attending Central Assembly of God in Bethlehem, Pennsylvania, when I was still little. I am not sure why she decided to start going to church, as up to this point, she lived a pretty hedonistic lifestyle. Maybe she was searching for stability, or perhaps she was desperate for positive community. Who knows, it could have been just God pulling her toward Him in a way she couldn't put into words. Whatever the reason, that decision rerouted the entire course of my story. That church became the place where she met Brian, the man who would become my dad. It became the place where, years later, I would walk my own bride down the aisle.

But before that future was secured, there was another hurdle to jump that the enemy put in my mom's and my path. Mike.

He was a friend of my dad's, part of the same church circle, I suppose. He dated my mother for a while, proposed to her, and for a stretch, it looked like they would be married. I have only fragments of memory of him, shadows of a face, glimpses of his presence at family gatherings. But one night at my grandparents' apartment in Northampton, the truth about him surfaced in a way that has never left me.

I don't know how other families operate, but when I was growing up, my family would get together a lot. Sometimes it was with all my aunts and uncles and their kids, and sometimes it would be more of my family going to visit my grandparents on our own. One evening, I found myself in the latter category, where my grandparents invited us over for dinner without everyone else there. My siblings and I were in the living room, watching cartoons on the TV. The adults sat in the dining room, their voices carrying through the doorway. I had a habit of listening in. Grown-up conversations always seemed more interesting than the cartoons. And that night in particular, the weight in everyone's voices pulled me in more.

I remember looking up and seeing my grandmother crying, my grandfather staring into his coffee cup, jaw tight. The words that spilled across that table were like poison in the air.

Mike had come to my grandparents' house recently to confess something dark and tragic. From what I recall and have been able to piece together, he was about to be arrested. He had been married, had children of his own, and was now facing charges for molesting his stepsons.

That was shocking enough on its own. But then he followed up with more information that could have gone unsaid, but I am oddly glad he offered it up. It has allowed me to gain access to another confirmational piece of the puzzle of my life, showing how supernaturally protected my life has been from an early age. What he had to say was something that chilled me to the bone even as a child, something I would carry with me the rest of my life.

Some nights before the night my family had visited, Mike sat across the table from my grandparents and admitted that when he had been engaged to my mother, he despised me. I was a toddler, not more than a year old, if that, at the time. He continued to tell them that if the marriage to my mother had gone through, I would have been the first to go.

When I overheard this information, I didn't know how to process it. I knew it was something to be fearful of, but I did not need to be afraid because Mike was no longer a threat in my life. He had not been for many years at this point. In our youth, we feel invincible, and receiving this news didn't change that for me. I had no clue how divinely protected I was. I don't think I even understood enough to fear what he meant. But God did.

Scripture tells us that *"The angel of the Lord encamps around those who fear him, and delivers them"* (Psalm 34:7 NIV). Before I even knew who God was, before I could fear Him in the biblical sense, He had already stationed His protection around my life. The same God who said, *"Before I formed you in the womb I knew you"* (Jeremiah 1:5 NIV), had plans for my life and needed me on a very particular path to become what He designed me to be. The Lord pulled me out of that trajectory before it ever had the chance to happen. He moved in my mother's heart, unsettled her, and gave her the courage to break off an engagement that would have destroyed me for the rest of my life.

I can still see my grandfather's face in that moment as he told my parents this information at the dining room table. He was brokenhearted, staring down into his coffee. Even though I wasn't his blood, I was his grandson. And he loved me fiercely.

That night left a mark. It taught me something about how God moves, about how the supernatural isn't always angels or visions. Sometimes it's a nudge in the human heart that changes everything. Sometimes it's God stepping in to reroute a story before evil can write its line. As Proverbs says, *"The king's heart is a stream of water in the hand of the Lord; he turns it wherever he will"* (Proverbs 21:1 ESV). If God can direct kings, He can certainly redirect a young mother's heart to protect her child.

And that's how I was grafted into the Merkel line, not by birth, but by design.

PAPPY'S MINISTRY AND MIRACLES

My grandfather was a preacher, but he never stood behind a pulpit week after week. He wasn't the kind of minister who had his name on a sign out front or an office with books stacked neatly on a desk. He was an ordained minister, yes, but he didn't pastor a church. His calling took a different shape.

He preached in men's groups, traveled with tent revivals, and led Bible studies inside prisons where the air was thick with regret. And somehow, that fit him. He wasn't a man coming from or seeking status of any kind. He was simply faithful to the call, wherever that may lead him. And God seemed to like using him that way. Jesus had said, *"...whoever would be great among you must be your servant"* (Mark 10:43 ESV), and that's exactly what my grandfather was—a servant.

From the time I was young, I knew there was something unusual about the way God moved around him. He never advertised it and never made a habit of retelling the same old glory stories of how God used him. He would never have wanted to be boastful in something that he couldn't claim ownership over. He knew where the true power lay—in the authority of Jesus Christ. But over time, the stories circulated anyway. Stories of blind eyes opening and stories of people rising out of wheelchairs. Even stories of demons shrieking and fleeing into the night.

When he grew sick and was diagnosed with cancer, I began visiting him in the hospital after work. It seemed like he was unlocking a safe that he had kept locked for many years. Inside this safe were many miraculous stories he was privileged to witness. One night during my visit, I brought a digital recorder because I wanted to capture some of those stories in his own voice. I didn't want the secondhand accounts of the stories. I wanted my children one day to hear it the way I had, directly from him.

One of the first stories he told me was about a girl he had prayed for at a revival. He couldn't even remember her face because there had been too many at that point. But later, a man asked if he remembered her, the girl who had been losing her sight, who was also going deaf. My grandfather shrugged. He couldn't place her. The man stared into his eyes with a stone-cold look. "Jack, she was healed. Sight back. Hearing back. Completely whole."

To me, my grandfather said it the way most people would mention the weather. No thematic music or emotional theatrics in the retelling. Just: It happened, and God did it. It reminded me of how the apostles spoke in Acts—not marveling at their own power, but simply stating, *"...why do you stare at us, as though by our own power or piety we have made him walk?"* (Acts 3:12 ESV).

THE FARMHOUSE

My grandfather told me about Tuesday nights at the Higgins farmhouse outside the town of New Tripoli in the Lehigh

Valley region of Pennsylvania. An old place with creaking floors and a warmth that came from more than the stove. He and my grandmother would drive in the car, and if no babysitter could be found, the kids came too. They'd set up chairs in a circle, nothing formal, and talk about the Lord. Somebody would start singing a hymn, and voices would rise off the wooden walls. Then prayer would break out, sometimes orderly, sometimes a flood.

The way he described it, the air in that farmhouse carried weight. Sometimes people were healed. Sometimes people fell to their knees in tears. Sometimes everyone just sat in silence because God's presence pressed down so heavily that no one wanted to break it. It was like those moments in Scripture when *"the priests could not perform their service because of the cloud, for the glory of the Lord filled the temple of God"* (2 Chronicles 5:14 NIV).

Those gatherings weren't about programs; instead, they were about expectancy. They taught my grandfather to anticipate that when you asked God to move, He just might. As Jesus promised, *"Where two or three are gathered in my name, there am I among them"* (Matthew 18:20 ESV).

As I think back on some of these stories, I wonder when was the last time I felt this sense of community. It seems like time moves faster than it did 50 years ago, and people have so much to do that we don't do what we were created to do—seek the Lord in as many ways as possible and as often as possible.

THE OIL TANK

Then there was the winter when the money ran out. My grandparents had five kids to raise on $50 a week. On top of that, some of that $50 went to child support for one of his older daughters, whom he loved dearly and no doubt happily supported. That left $40 to stretch across everything else.

The house they lived in had once been a barn, which was drafty and cold, and one winter the fuel oil tank in the basement was running low. The gauge showed a quarter tank left, and there was no money to refill it.

So in desperate faith, my grandfather prayed. He laid his hands on that steel tank and asked God to stretch it. "Lord, I don't have it," he prayed. "You kept the oil in the lamps burning for eight days in Jerusalem. Do it for me here."

For the next week and a half, the needle never moved. Outside, the temperature stayed in the low twenties. But the house stayed warm. That quarter tank carried them until more money came in.

He told the story without drama. But I could feel the gratitude in his voice, the kind that only comes from watching God step into your lack and meet it head-on time and time again. It was the widow's oil that wouldn't run out (1 Kings 17:14-16), the five loaves and two fish that fed thousands (Matthew 14:17-21). The same God who multiplied then was multiplying now.

THE WOMAN IN THE PRAYER LINE

Then there was the woman who came forward for prayer at a campground service. This woman's eyes were wild and her movements restless. My grandmother noticed her first. "Something was wrong in her eyes," she said later. "I have seen eyes like this myself, and you know, there is something else in control of a person when you see them."

The woman looked at my grandfather and asked what he could do for her, and no doubt offered prayer since they were in a prayer line. She sneered at the very idea of prayer. "What's prayer going to do for me?"

He didn't feel he had an answer that would cut through the darkness he saw in her. So he prayed silently for help. "Lord, I don't know what to say to her."

And in his spirit, he heard the response: "Ask her about the blood."

So he did. "Do you know about the blood?"

The woman recoiled. He pressed again, "What about the blood?"

She grew physically irritated and frantic, her face contorting as she stammered for words.

He leaned in, "What about the blood?"

Each time he asked, something inside her seemed to squirm. Over and over again. Back and forth they went, and then all of a sudden, it broke.

She let out a scream that ripped across the campground like a siren. People on the hill heard it and came running as she bolted and collapsed in the field beyond the tent where the service was being held.

The only thing that cut through her torment was the blood of Jesus. The same blood that has silenced demons since the Cross. As Scripture says, *"They have conquered him by the blood of the Lamb..."* (Revelation 12:11 ESV). My grandfather never told these stories to make himself sound powerful. He said it to point to the truth: there is still power in the blood. There always has been and there always will be.

That was the man I grew up under. A quiet and faithful man. A man who prayed expecting Heaven to answer.

And all of those stories, powerful as they were, were leading toward the One who has echoed in me more than any other. The night when angels themselves stood guard at the edge of a Pennsylvania campground.

THE NIGHT THE ANGELS STOOD GUARD

It was the summer of 1976, Fourth of July weekend. My grandparents had loaded the kids into the car and driven out to the campground, just like they did nearly every weekend. By then, it had become a rhythm of their lives. Friday night services under the tent at the top of the hill, Saturday gatherings around the pavilion, Sunday mornings filled with preaching and worship.

I imagine the tent stood like a beacon, glowing under stringed lights, music pouring out into the night with voices lifted in worship. Children running around through the grass, and somewhere a pavilion filled with the smell of grilled food and the chatter of families swapping stories, while the kids darted in and out of the shadows.

But not everyone welcomed the sight of that tent. Some in the community didn't want revival breaking out in their backyard. I am willing to bet that these people didn't know where the root source of their animosity came from, but it was, without a doubt, fueled by demonic principalities. As Paul wrote, *"We do not wrestle against flesh and blood, but against the rulers, against the authorities, against the cosmic powers over this present darkness..."* (Ephesians 6:12 ESV). That summer, rumors spread that a group of men planned to storm the campground one night to cause trouble and rip down the tent.

And on that Fourth of July weekend, it felt like the rumors had finally come due.

The service had ended earlier than usual. The families gathered under the pavilion, waiting. Conversation dropped to low tones. Every sound beyond the tree line made heads turn. The children sensed the tension, sticking close to their parents. My grandfather and a few of the men kept watch, determined not to let fear run them off.

Then the headlights appeared at the entrance.

A car rolled up slowly, gravel crunching beneath its tires. The car stopped somewhere on the driveway and just idled. The pavilion grew silent. Everyone waited for the doors to fly open, for shouts to break out, for violence to erupt.

But nothing happened. The car just sat there idling for what seemed to be several minutes, then it backed away and drove off.

Confused and not knowing what to make of the odd encounter, people surely went back to their conversations with kids playing around the pavilion. But not long after, another set of headlights appeared coming down the driveway. This time, multiple cars. This time it was the same as the last, but with two cars. The cars approached, engines rumbling in the night. They paused at the entrance as if weighing their options, and then, without explanation, they turned around and left.

This happened several more times, each time with more cars appearing than the previous time.

Car after car crept toward the campground, but not one of them crossed a certain threshold.

The people under the pavilion held their ground, praying under their breath and refusing to scatter. Over time, slowly, the night went quiet. No raid. No fight. Just silence and confusion.

Here's where the story takes on biblical proportions. There's a passage in 2 Kings that I can't help but connect to what happened that night. The prophet Elisha and his servant were surrounded by an enemy army sent to capture them. The servant panicked, seeing they were vastly outnumbered. But Elisha remained calm and prayed, *"O Lord, please open his eyes that he may see."* And Scripture records: *"So the Lord opened the eyes of the young man, and he saw, and behold, the mountain was full of horses and chariots of fire all around Elisha"* (2 Kings 6:17 ESV).

The servant's problem wasn't that they were outnumbered. It was that he couldn't see the full picture. The supernatural army of God had been there all along, invisible to natural eyes but absolutely real, absolutely present, absolutely protective.

That's exactly what happened at that Pennsylvania campground.

The next day, the explanation arrived. My grandfather said this must have been the talk of the town, the way it spread. Someone who had been among the group planning to storm the campground told others in town what happened. They said the men had driven out there ready to cause chaos and destroy the place. But when they reached the entrance, they froze because standing across the field were figures that were towering, immovable, and shoulder to shoulder. Angels.

They stretched across the road like a living wall, blazing with the kind of presence that makes grown men tremble. Not one of these cars filled with people would even attempt to pass by them. It must have gotten to a point where people were coming to see the spectacle and probably forgot that they wanted to cause harm in the first place.

I often try to picture that scene with the headlights cutting across the gravel, catching the shimmer of something otherworldly. Hardened men, bold enough to plan an attack, suddenly gripped by terror at the sight of Heaven's warriors standing guard. And all they could do was turn their cars around and flee into the night.

Just like Elisha's servant, the believers under that pavilion couldn't see the angels. They were left in the dark, literally and figuratively. But their prayers had been answered. God had sent His army. As the psalmist declared, *"He will command his angels concerning you to guard you in all your ways"* (Psalm 91:11 ESV).

When my grandfather told me that story, his voice carried no doubt, even though he and his companions never saw the angels. They were left to trust, to pray, to stand firm. If it had not been for the rumors spreading all over town in such a short span of time, he may have never known what happened that night.

For him, it was one more story among many. For me, it became a pillar of proof that the God I had been taught about wasn't confined to church buildings and sermons. He was here with us and highly active. And when His people are in danger, He will send His armies to stand between them and the darkness.

That night became more than a family story; it became a seed planted in me. Long before I would have language for it, long before I'd be sitting across from people telling me about UFOs, dogmen, or demons, I already knew this: there is more happening in the unseen realm than we realize. And sometimes, if you're paying attention, you catch a glimpse of it.

THE MANTLE

Years later, long after my grandfather had passed, I received a phone call from my aunt Ellen, just a few weeks ago from writing this, actually. She wasn't calling to chat; from the moment I heard her voice, I could tell she had something pressing on her spirit.

She told me about a season after Pappy's death when she was involved in a charismatic church in Buffalo, New York. It was the kind of place where prophets and prophetesses moved freely, calling out people and speaking words over them. She explained that she had always been cautious about things like that, because Pappy had raised her to test everything against Scripture. "Take it with a grain of salt," he'd say. "Go home, open your Bible, and if it matches, receive it. If not, let it go." That was his steady, grounded way. As John wrote, "*…test the spirits to see whether they are from God…*" (1 John 4:1 ESV).

But one night, a prophetess walked straight up to her and said, "You're a seer. The Lord shows you things. When He tells you something, you need to speak it. If you hold back, you're holding back someone else's blessing."

It startled her because she had always known, deep down, that she sometimes sensed things others couldn't. Whether it be a word, a knowing, or an impression she couldn't explain. But she had always kept that understanding to herself as she was afraid of being misunderstood or judged by people around her.

However, that moment seemed to have cracked something open in her. She has been watching and observing me from a distance. It had been years of no communication between my aunt and I as we live in different states and have our own lives. But she has been seeing me step more publicly into ministry as I operate under my own callings and convictions from my Lord and Savior. She knew she couldn't hold back information on what she had been "seeing" any longer.

"Anthony," she said, "the mantle that Pappy carried hasn't vanished. It's been lying there waiting to be picked up, and the Lord is putting it on you."

The biblical precedent hit me immediately. When Elijah was taken up to Heaven, his mantle fell to the ground, and Elisha picked it up. With it came a double portion of Elijah's spirit—not because Elisha was blood related to Elijah, but because God had chosen him for the succession (2 Kings 2:13-14). The mantle wasn't about genetics; it was about calling.

Aunt Ellen reminded me of what she had seen with her own eyes when she was young. Blind people receiving their sight, deaf people hearing again, a man rising from a wheelchair, and demons screaming and fleeing at the name of Jesus. She told me how humble Pappy had been through all of it, never puffing himself up, never claiming credit, and always pointing to what God had done.

And now she was telling me that the mantle wasn't buried with him, it was dormant. It was waiting. And she believed I was the one God had chosen to pick it up.

Her words hit me like a ton of bricks falling from Heaven itself. Out of all the grandchildren, the ones with his blood running through their veins, she was saying it was me. The one without a biological tie. The one grafted in.

I couldn't help but ask the question that had haunted me for years: "Why me?"

Her answer was simple. "Because God said so. Because you've already been marked for it."

I sat there with the phone pressed to my ear, her words replaying in my head. All my life, I had wrestled with why God had grafted me into this family line. Why me, when I didn't even share the bloodline? Why was I the one carrying the stories, the memories, the weight? And now she was telling me plainly: it wasn't random. It was an assignment.

Paul wrote to the Romans about being grafted into the olive tree: *"If some of the branches were broken off, and you, although a wild olive shoot, were grafted in among the others and now share in the nourishing root of the olive tree"* (Romans 11:17 ESV). That was me—a wild olive shoot, grafted into a spiritual lineage not by blood but by divine design.

GUARDIAN OF THE FRONTIER

The morning after that call with Aunt Ellen, I sat across the kitchen table from my wife, replaying the conversation. I told her about the mantle, about Pappy's miracles, about the things Aunt Ellen had seen with her own eyes. And I confessed the question that had gnawed at me for years: Why me? Of all the grandchildren, why was I the one? I wasn't even blood.

The question hung in the air until my wife leaned forward and asked, "What about the name?"

I'd never paid the name Merkel much mind—I thought it sounded odd, clunky. Approaching 40, I'd collected four last names attached to my life: Diaz (my biological father), Ohlinger (my mother's maiden name), Frickert (the name I carried through tenth grade), and now Merkel.

From the day I was born it was obvious my biological father wouldn't be part of my life, and my mom didn't want to saddle me with his name. She wrestled with what identity to give her firstborn. Something in her knew a name carried weight. She couldn't bring herself to use Ohlinger either—it was the name of the stepfather who adopted her, then abused her, and whom she hadn't spoken to since she was 12 years old. So she did the next most reasonable thing: she gave me my great-grandmother's maiden name, Frickert. Imagine a brown Puerto Rican kid growing up in the sticks of Pennsylvania Dutch country with the last name Frickert—I stuck out like a sore thumb. I felt like a misfit from the start.

It wasn't until tenth grade that the courts finally allowed my dad, Brian, to adopt me and for me to take the name Merkel. They'd been trying for years, but without my biological father's signature, the paperwork wouldn't go through. That's how it felt sometimes—like the ownership of my person and identity was being transacted from one family tree to the next. So when I say I never really thought about Merkel, I mean it. I'd been tied to so many family names and the histories they carried that they blended together into one identity: a mutt.

Maybe something inside me had kept me from digging deeper into what this new tree actually meant.

Growing up, I was told Merkel meant "merchant." A merchant. A trader. Selling baskets in some old-world market. It felt cheap and untrue to the weight I sensed in my life. That shallow meaning only reinforced the idea that I didn't belong anywhere—that I was rootless at my core.

My wife opened her laptop and started digging past the surface. She said she couldn't find "merchant" linked to Merkel, then stopped, eyes wide. She read the words that folded the room in on itself: "Guardian of the Frontier."

Those words hit like a revelation. The kitchen went quiet. My mind left the table—I was on a street corner preaching the gospel, I was in my studio pulling back the curtain on evil, I was standing behind a pulpit sharing my testimony to wake the Church from its slumber. I was on a wind-blown hill screaming that a supernatural war raged all around us—two worlds battling for human souls. The phrase carried me into the future and the past, to faraway listeners receiving a message they didn't know they needed.

Guardian of the Frontier. It didn't just fit—it explained. It explained the pull I'd always felt toward the unseen, the places people were afraid to look. It explained why God placed me in a strange calling with *The Confessionals* (my podcast), why I stand at the edge of the abyss listening to stories most churches would rather ignore.

I'd been doing it without realizing it: standing in the gap between worlds, holding the line between light and darkness. Like the watchmen on the walls in ancient Israel who were commanded: *"I have set watchmen upon thy walls, O Jerusalem, which shall never hold their peace day nor night…"* (Isaiah 62:6 KJV).

I shook my head and let out a soft laugh. "Of course," I said. "That's it." God had designed me to be a Merkel. Not a Diaz. Not an Ohlinger. Not a Frickert. A Merkel—and God knew it before I was in my mother's womb. As He told Jeremiah: *"Before I formed you in the womb I knew you, and before you were born I consecrated you…"* (Jeremiah 1:5 ESV).

But it didn't stop there. I asked my wife to look up her maiden name, Garrett. She scrolled and read aloud: "Spear-Bearer."

The two names hung between us: Guardian of the Frontier, married to a Spear-Bearer.

I sat back, stunned. God hadn't just grafted me into the Merkel line; He had paired me with someone whose very name meant she was to help arm me for battle. For 18 years, she had been my encourager and my anchor—quiet with words but steady in action. She is the one who hands me the ammunition when the fight presses in: the shield in one hand, the spear in the other, silently equipping the army.

GUARDIAN AND SPEAR-BEARER

It felt almost too perfect, like God had left breadcrumbs in our names to find at just the right moment. Once I saw it, I couldn't unsee it. This wasn't random. This was an assignment. As Psalm 139:16 (ESV) declares: *"Your eyes saw my unformed substance; in your book were written, every one of them, the days that were formed for me, when as yet there was none of them."*

All my life, I'd wrestled with not being blood, wondering why I was grafted into this family line. Now I had an answer. I hadn't merely been adopted into a name—I had been placed there by God. Positioned to pick up a mantle that was set down by the one who came before me. Paired with a wife who would stand beside me in the fight.

This was more than family history. This was identity.

THE WEIGHT OF INHERITANCE

After the call with Aunt Ellen and this new revelation of my name, I knew something I had never dared to say out loud—my life had been marked from the beginning.

It started the night God pulled me out of the trajectory with Mike—the man who admitted I would have been his first victim. It continued in the way my grandfather claimed me as his own, not by blood, but by love and calling. It showed up in the stories of healings and deliverances, in the farmhouse prayer meetings where the Spirit pressed down heavily, in the oil tank that never ran dry. It climaxed in that campground when angels stood guard at the gate and sent men home trembling in the dark.

And it didn't stop when my grandfather's body failed. Even on his deathbed, his hand tried to squeeze mine with the last strength he had as he was hours away from taking his last breath. With that last hand squeeze, something passed from him to me. A mantle. A weight. A calling.

My aunt only confirmed it years later when she said what I had always felt but never named: It's yours now. God is putting it on you.

And then came the revelation of the name itself—Merkel, Guardian of the Frontier. I had spent years asking why I, of all the grandchildren, was chosen to carry this weight. Why was I grafted into this family line? And God answered in a way only He could. I wasn't just placed here—I was named for it.

Guardian of the Frontier. Spear-Bearer at my side.

It was never random. It was by design.

But here's what you need to understand—this isn't just my story. The spiritual war I'm describing, the inheritance I'm talking about, the battles between seen and unseen—you're in this too. Whether you know it or not, whether you believe it or not, you were born into the same battlefield. The question isn't whether you're in the war. The question is whether you're fighting with Heaven's army or standing exposed and alone.

I didn't ask for this mantle. I didn't go looking for it. But I can't escape it either. In some ways, you could say it chased me down. My inheritance isn't just family memories—it's a mantle forged in prayer, miracles, and angelic fire. And that mantle demands something of me.

Because if these stories are true—and I believe they are—then I've been handed more than nostalgia. I've been handed a weapon. A role to play in a war that's older than my bloodline, older than my family name, older than the world itself.

I didn't understand it all at the time. Honestly, I still don't. But I know this much: the war is real. The frontier is thin. And I have no choice now but to stand my ground.

What I didn't know then was how desperately I would try to run from this calling, but even as I wrestled with this inheritance, I began to sense something larger at work. The same supernatural reality that had touched my grandfather's ministry was still active—not just in my family line, but everywhere. People worldwide were having encounters that defied explanation, left alone with experiences that terrified them because no one would believe their stories.

What I wouldn't understand until much later was that these encounters—the UFO from my childhood, the demons my grandfather cast out, the angels at the campground—weren't random supernatural events. They were all part of the same ancient war, different masks worn by the same rebellion. The enemy's tactics had evolved, but the goal remained unchanged: separate humanity from truth through confusion, fear, and deception.

The mantle waiting for me wasn't just about healing prayers or tent revivals. It was about standing at that thin place where worlds collide, bearing witness to the evidence, helping others understand what they're really facing. Whether someone encounters a creature in the woods, lights in the sky, or shadows in their room, they're glimpsing the same conflict that's been raging since Eden.

But first, I would have to learn the hard way what happens when you step into spiritual territory without understanding your inheritance—when you try to fight battles in your own strength instead of God's authority.

3
THE HOLLOW FRAME

When my father and my mother forsake me, then the Lord will take me up.

—Psalm 27:10 KJV

That's the inheritance I carry now—Guardian of the Frontier, paired with my Spear-Bearer. But I need to back up and tell you what happened between my grandfather's death and that phone call with Aunt Ellen. Because I almost lost it all before I ever understood what it meant.

I would love to tell you that when my grandfather died, I stood strong in faith. But that would be a lie.

The truth is, my grandfather had been a spiritual crutch in my life. When he was alive, I leaned on him without even realizing how much. His presence was like a covering, a steady force that gave me confidence in what I thought was my own walk with God. But when he was gone, I discovered something devastating: my faith had been borrowed. It wasn't mine. It was like somebody ripped the foundation out from under me and left me standing on a hollow frame that was ready to collapse.

At the time, I didn't know about mantles or spiritual inheritance or any of that. I wouldn't understand for years that something had been set down, waiting to be picked up. All I knew was that something essential had been ripped away, and I was stumbling in the dark trying to find my footing.

There was a gaping hole in my family after he passed. We all felt it. He had been the glue that kept everyone together, the one who stood in the gap, prayed the prayers, and carried an authority that seemed to blanket us whether we noticed it or not. Without that covering, we were exposed. And one by one, different members of the family started taking hits. Some of those hits were subtle, some were heavy, but they came.

During this vulnerable time, God tried to warn me. One night, I had a dream that I believed at the time was demonic. But years later, I came to understand it was actually a warning from God about the danger I was in.

In the dream, I was in my home church in Kutztown, Pennsylvania—a small church that sat on top of a hill on the outskirts of town, surrounded by cornfields. I was bouncing down the stairs with that light, familiar energy you have when you know a place by heart. I opened the door to the basement where they held receptions and potlucks, a large gathering hall with a kitchen.

As I stood in the doorway, the kitchen was in front of me, the gathering hall to my right, and to my left were bathrooms and the church office. Everything was exactly as it was in real life. But then I saw my dad standing in the gathering hall in his Sunday dress attire, staring dead ahead toward the church office.

"Hey Dad, what's going on?" I asked.

He didn't move. Didn't even flinch. Didn't acknowledge I was there. It was as if he were an empty drone, a robot waiting to be powered up.

As I stood there confused, I looked to where he was staring. The office to my left grew dark—not just absence of light, but a supernatural black darkness, like a black substance or mist forming in the room. Suddenly, the whole space shifted. The room expanded. The office that had been 6 feet away was now 20 or 30 feet away. My dad was farther away on my right. I had become smaller in the space.

From that black cloud came something that still chills me to remember: black demonic hands crawling across the floor, grabbing at the ground to pull themselves toward me. The darkness was coming for me.

I looked to my dad, still standing there with that dead stare. "Dad! Dad!" I yelled. Nothing. He just kept staring as if he wasn't even there.

The arms and the black cloud reached me, grabbed me, pulled me to the ground. They started dragging me back toward that church office. I was screaming, "Dad, please help me! Dad, help me! Dad, please help me!"

Nothing. He just stood there staring as if I wasn't even there.

As those arms pulled me into the church office, I woke up.

For years, I thought this was a demonic attack dream, sent from the enemy to scare me. It wasn't until much later, after going through tremendous spiritual struggles, that I realized God had been warning me. I had been using my parents' spiritual walk—my dad's faith, my grandfather's anointing, the faith of those around me—as a substitute for my own relationship with Jesus Christ. I lived a Christian life through association, not transformation. I had never truly yielded my heart to the Lord but rather lived vicariously through others.

The dream was showing me what would happen when those supports couldn't help me anymore. When the darkness came, their faith couldn't save me. I needed my own.

But I didn't understand the warning then. Instead, I just kept stumbling forward, trying to build a life on that hollow frame.

THE COUNTERFEIT FOUNDATION

It was in that fragile season when Lindsay and I started dating.

I was 18 years old. We had known each other since middle school, but I hadn't really noticed her until the summer after my first year of Bible college. I came home, walked into church one Sunday, and there she was. Something inside of me clicked. I recognized her, but I saw her for the first time.

Looking back, I think part of what drew me to Lindsay was that she represented stability. She had her own genuine faith. Maybe subconsciously, I thought if I attached myself to her, I could keep borrowing faith from someone else. Solomon wrote: *"Two are better than one...if they fall, one will lift up his fellow. But woe to him who is alone when he falls and has not another to lift him up!"* (Ecclesiastes 4:9-10 ESV). But I was about to learn that even the best human relationship can't substitute for a relationship with God.

The way I fell for Lindsay was immediate and complete. I remember driving home with my dad after church on a Sunday, and we were going through the parking lot when Lindsay was walking from her 2000 Ford Focus back into the church. As she walked across the pavement, I told my dad she was the most beautiful girl I'd ever seen in my life. I'd recently sworn off dating after some unfavorable relationships, but once I saw her, all bets were off. My dad will tell you that when I said that, he looked across the car at me and knew I was already gone.

Within weeks I was telling the guys at church that I was going to marry her. They laughed it off, but I was dead serious. By the grace of God, she gave me a chance. And even more than that, she fell in love with me too.

We got married at age 21. We were young. We didn't have life figured out. But we were determined. What I didn't understand then was that my brain literally wasn't finished developing. Scientists tell us that a man's brain doesn't fully mature until around 25. I was four years away from a fully developed prefrontal cortex—the part that handles impulse control, long-term planning, and emotional regulation. Looking back, it showed in every decision I made.

The problem was that, almost immediately after the honeymoon excitement wore off, marriage started to feel like the wrong decision. Not because Lindsay wasn't amazing—she was. But because I was trying to build on a foundation that didn't exist. *"Unless the Lord builds the house, those who build it labor in vain…"* (Psalm 127:1 ESV). I was laboring in vain, and I didn't even know it.

Most of our arguments were my fault. I was immature, hotheaded, and damaged. I carried childhood wounds into my marriage, and they came out sharp. At 21, I was trying to figure out who I was while also trying to figure out how to be a husband.

I remember scrolling through Facebook, seeing photos of guys from high school out partying, living it up. I was sitting in a 700-square-foot apartment with my wife, and resentment ate at me. I thought we married too young, that I was missing out.

The real issue wasn't my age or circumstances. The real issue was that I had no spiritual foundation. I was like the man Jesus described who built his house on sand: *"And the rain fell, and the floods came, and the winds blew and beat against that house, and it fell, and great was the fall of it"* (Matthew 7:27 ESV). The storms were coming, and I had nothing to anchor me.

I bounced from job to job, restless and unsettled. Auto garage, school buses, and various CDL jobs. I was becoming a product of whatever environment I found myself in. If I were around good men, I could fake it. But if I were in a rough environment, I would slide right into it without resistance. Paul's warning was playing out in my life: *"Do not be deceived: Bad company ruins good morals"* (1 Corinthians 15:33 ESV).

One of the biggest battles was over my wedding ring. I'd take it off for work, claiming it got in the way. But "forgetting" became a pattern. Weeks would pass without wearing it. Lindsay knew what it meant. That ring was a covenant symbol, and removing it was my way of rejecting the weight of commitment. Like Esau, who *"despised his birthright"* for temporary comfort (Genesis 25:34 ESV), I was trading covenant for convenience.

THE DESCENT

Then basketball pulled me back in. Coaching gave me something that felt like purpose. I got into the best shape of my life, and with that came attention—or at least I perceived it that way. My ego fed on it. Pride swelled. The more my ego grew, the more distance I put between Lindsay and me.

I didn't want to admit it, but I wanted out of my marriage. Instead of having the courage to leave, I did something more cowardly: I tried to make her life miserable enough that she would leave me. Then I could play the victim.

I started drinking more. Stayed out late. Found any excuse to create distance. Proverbs says, *"Pride goes before destruction, and a haughty spirit before a fall"* (Proverbs 16:18 ESV). I was careening toward both.

One night, I came home around one in the morning after drinking with friends. Lindsay was waiting at the kitchen table with a letter.

Two things in that letter broke through my walls.

First: "If we get a divorce, it won't be because I divorced you. It will be because you divorced me." She saw through my game.

Second: "When you go to bed at night, I know you still love me. Because even in your sleep, you roll over and put your arm around me."

She was right. Somewhere beneath all the self-destruction, love remained. But I was so full of self-hatred that I couldn't receive the love she offered. *"There is no fear in love, but perfect love casts out fear…"* (1 John 4:18 ESV). I was too full of fear to let love in.

That letter cracked something open. I quit basketball, knowing it fed my ego. I turned to trucking—12 to 14 hours alone on the road. In some ways, it saved my marriage by removing temptation. But I was still running from God.

One day at a fuel stop, an older driver named George watched me berate someone over nothing. He looked at me with tired eyes: "You're one mean person."

His words haunted me. The bullied had become the bully. I decided to change, forcing myself to say nice things, small improvements that cost enormous effort. But I was trying to transform myself without the Transformer. As Jesus said, "*...apart from me you can do nothing*" (John 15:5 ESV).

THE ENCOUNTER

During this time, Lindsay's great-uncle passed away. His funeral was the same day as my friend Zach's wedding—Zach was the son of Pastor Winters, who I'd grown up under at my home church. I'd known Zach since childhood; our families were close. The wedding would be a reunion of sorts, filled with people from my past. I wanted the wedding—joy over grief, celebration over sorrow. But Lindsay wanted me at the funeral. Because I loved her, despite the dysfunction, I chose her over myself.

That decision changed everything.

The funeral was in an old red brick church. Most of the service was predictable—until Lindsay's uncle Dave stood up. He was a Baptist pastor from Maine who had come for the funeral. He wasn't on the program, but something moved him. With visible frustration, he looked at the minister leading the service and said, "If no one else is going to do it, then I'll do it."

And he preached the gospel.

I'd heard it hundreds of times, but that day it hit like fire. Not because of the words, but because of how much I hated hearing them. Rage boiled up. I was furious at him, at God, at myself.

Then the atmosphere shifted. Everything blurred except for this singular moment. I was locked in, frozen, singled out.

And God spoke.

For the first time in my life, I heard the Holy Spirit's voice—not audible, but unmistakable.

"You don't need to change to come to Me. Just come to Me, and I'll change you."

I had been trying to change myself for months. Trying to fix my marriage. Trying to be better. But never once had I considered that I couldn't do it alone. God wasn't asking me to clean myself up first. He was inviting me to come as I was—broken, angry, prideful—and let Him do the transformation. *"Therefore, if anyone is in Christ, he is a new creation. The old has passed away; behold, the new has come"* (2 Corinthians 5:17 ESV).

I walked out of that church a different person. We went straight to the wedding reception—the one for the wedding I had skipped to attend the funeral. This wasn't just any wedding—it was Pastor Winters' son, from the church I'd grown up in. My whole family was there, which is why they were all at the reception. Standing with my parents, my brother Jack, my sister Tanya, and Lindsay at the end of the night, I broke. When my dad asked about the funeral, I told them everything. Tears, sobbing, confession. It was my prodigal son moment: *"This my son was dead, and is alive again; he was lost, and is found..."* (Luke 15:24 KJV).

Everyone cried. They knew what kind of man I had been and saw that something had fundamentally changed. That night, I truly gave my life to Jesus Christ. Not through association, not through borrowed faith, but personally, genuinely, completely.

THE FIRE AND THE GAP

The days that followed burned with holy fire. I couldn't get enough of God. Driving truck with sermons playing, waking early to read Scripture, sitting on the floor at night scrolling through Bible verses. Nobody forced me. It was pure hunger.

"As a deer pants for flowing streams, so pants my soul for you, O God" (Psalm 42:1 ESV).

An evangelist was being born in me. I wanted to share the gospel with everyone. The fire was too strong to contain.

But here's what I didn't understand then: I had accepted Christ, but I was still operating in my own strength. I didn't know about the spiritual inheritance waiting for me. I didn't know about the mantle that had been set down when my grandfather died. I didn't know that God had more for me than just salvation—He had a calling, an assignment, a place in the spiritual battle.

And because I didn't know, I was still vulnerable. When you step into spiritual territory in your own power, when you try to do God's work without God's full equipping, you become a target. The enemy sees the gap in your armor and aims for it.

I thought my zeal would be enough. I thought the fire of new conversion was all the protection I needed. But enthusiasm isn't armor, and good intentions aren't the same as spiritual authority. I was about to learn that salvation is free, but walking in spiritual authority requires surrender to the full calling God has for you—even the parts you don't know about yet.

The encounter with the satanist that was coming would teach me that lesson the hard way. But first, I would ride that wave of evangelistic fire, mistaking my passion for power, my excitement for equipment. I was like a soldier running into battle with a torch but no sword, light but no armor.

Jay would be waiting. And I would walk right into his trap, carrying nothing but a Bible and the naive confidence of someone who didn't yet understand that the enemy studies our weaknesses and sets his snares accordingly.

4

The Trap

Be sober-minded; be watchful. Your adversary the devil prowls around like a roaring lion, seeking someone to devour.

—1 Peter 5:8 ESV

After my radical conversion back to Christ, I couldn't help but talk about Jesus everywhere. The Lord had hit me like a freight train. Within a week or two, I found myself bubbling with that almost embarrassing joy that pours up and floods your face without asking permission. I couldn't contain it. I was on a spiritual high like I'd never experienced. The Holy Spirit was speaking to me so clearly in those days that when He said something, I didn't even question it—I just knew it would happen. I'd go home and tell Lindsay, "God told me this today," and ask her to be a witness for when it came to pass.

I was suddenly the guy who wanted to talk, who wanted to ask real questions. I started staying longer at delivery docks, not because my route demanded it but because the men who unloaded me turned into stories I couldn't put down.

There was this one place I hit regularly. Same building, same guy at the dock—let's call him Jay. Between straps and pallets, he began handing me chapters of his life. Every time I pulled in, he'd be there like a book somebody had left open, and he would tell me something new. His life read like a slow confession, bits of hurt and grit, and he told it like he was aching for somebody to hear it.

It was a Tuesday when everything shifted. We were up to current times in his story, and it was getting depressing. I asked him a simple question—the one that feels like it could flip a life over: "What's next for you?"

He looked at me like I'd asked him the weather, turned his head sideways like a dog, and then said, plain as a flatline, "I don't know, probably just blow my brains out."

That's what broke something loose in me. The evangelist in me rose up. "No," I said. "You don't want to do that. God's got plans for your life."

The way he questioned me after that, it was like he'd never heard of God. Not in the casual way of someone who doesn't go to church, but like the word was foreign to him. He asked questions that made me feel like I had stepped into an alternate United States of America. How does someone grow up here and not even know who Jesus is? Not just not believing, but literally not knowing?

He followed me out to my truck, hungry for more. "I really want to talk to you more about this God," he said. So we exchanged information—he only had a landline and an email, no cell phone—and I scheduled right there to come to his house that Saturday at 11 a.m. to talk about God.

I left thinking: cake walk, done. This guy is getting saved.

THE WEEK OF WARNING

The whole week I started out rejoicing. "Thank You, God," I prayed. "We're going to add to the Kingdom on Saturday." But as the week went on, the Holy Spirit started speaking to me, preparing my inner soul for very heavy, dark spiritual warfare.

I tried to dismiss it. "No, you're wrong. This guy is primed to accept Jesus. He's going to come to salvation on Saturday. I got this covered."

But the feeling got stronger and stronger. By Friday, even Lindsay was feeling it. She hadn't even told me she was sensing something. But that Saturday morning, she demanded I give her Jay's address, his phone number, and when I'd be back. "If you're not back by a certain time, I'm calling the police," she said.

I tried to play it off. "What are you talking about? It's going to be a rejoicing time." But inside, I was starting to feel the weight of what God had been warning me about.

I stopped at church to pick up a Bible for Jay. I told my pastor I felt God warning me about serious spiritual warfare. He tried to rationalize it: "Well, every time somebody comes to the Lord, there's spiritual warfare."

"This feels darker," I said.

We prayed, and I went on my way.

Paul warned the Corinthians: *"For such men are false apostles, deceitful workmen, disguising themselves as apostles of Christ. And no wonder, for even Satan disguises himself as an angel of light"* (2 Corinthians 11:13-14). But I was too new, too eager, too high on my own spiritual mountaintop to recognize a trap when I was walking into one.

THE HOUSE OF DARKNESS

I knocked at his door at 11 a.m., just like I said I would. Nobody answered at first. I knocked again, and then the door slowly opened by itself. It was completely black inside. I peeked my head in without entering and said hello.

Jay stepped out from behind the door. "You showed up?"

"Yeah, I showed up. I told you I'd show up."

"Most people don't show up."

Right there, my brain should have caught that. Most people? Like he'd done this before? But it went right over my head.

The living room was wallpapered with pin-up girls from floor to ceiling on every wall. Not like a college dorm, but like it was the actual wallpaper. My first thought: this guy's definitely single. No woman would tolerate this.

He said we could sit at the dining room table. The layout was a townhouse—I walked into the living room, and then the dining room was on the other side, with a built-in bookshelf that extended out from the wall to separate the two rooms. As I walked past the bookshelf, the Holy Spirit tugged at me: be aware of the bookshelf.

Then as I approached the table, the Holy Spirit spoke again, fast and specific: sit in the chair to the left, between the table and the window, not the chair between the table and the door that led to the basement.

THE THREE-HOUR RITUAL

We started talking—this wasn't a quick conversation; it was a three-hour ordeal. We went back and forth between the dining room and his kitchen, which he'd converted into a workshop for building RC cars. He'd smoke in the kitchen but not the dining room, for whatever reason. His diet consisted of Mountain Dew, Doritos, and ramen noodles. He said physically he couldn't eat anything else.

We talked about random things at first. I mentioned I had a group called Pennsylvania Sasquatch Research, and he talked about making an RC car for it. Just casual conversation while I waited for the right moment to shift toward God.

Then he asked me, "Do you believe in ghosts?"

This was before I had my podcast, before I really thought about this stuff. I was Bigfoot guy, not ghost guy. But something inside—maybe God—said, *Okay, here it comes.*

"Yeah, I believe in ghosts," I said. "I mean, in the Bible they thought Jesus was a ghost walking on water, so I guess there's some merit to it."

"Okay," he said. "There are seven ghosts in this house."

Scripture says, *"When the unclean spirit has gone out of a person, it passes through waterless places seeking rest, but finds none. Then it says, 'I will return to my house from which I came.' And when it comes, it finds the house empty, swept, and put in order. Then it goes and brings with it seven other spirits more evil than itself..."* (Matthew 12:43-45 ESV). Seven spirits. The number wasn't random.

He started talking about where the ghosts came from, something about the basement. "You want to come down and see?" he asked, gesturing toward that door God had told me not to sit in front of.

Back then I was less confident as a man, not one to challenge somebody in their own home. But I looked at him seriously and said, "No, we're going to stay up here."

He shrugged. "Okay."

Part of me wishes we had gone down, just to see what was there. But I don't know if I would have made it back out.

We started talking about God, and I shared who Jesus Christ was. Jay started physically shaking in his seat, rocking back and forth in agreement, like he wanted to jump out of his chair. My ego kicked in—this is it, he's about to get saved!

"You're clearly ready," I said. "Are you ready to accept Christ in your life today?"

"Yes."

"All right, let's do this."

We prayed a simple prayer. After I said amen, he stood up and started pacing back and forth, shaking his hands violently. "I feel this energy rushing through my body!"

That's new, I thought. I'd done street ministry back in Bible college—talking to drug dealers and drunks coming out of bars at midnight—but I'd never seen that reaction. But God does mysterious things, right?

The apostle John warned us: *"Beloved, do not believe every spirit, but test the spirits to see whether they are from God..."* (1 John 4:1 ESV). Real encounters with the Holy Spirit bring peace, joy, self-control—fruits of the Spirit, not violent shaking and strange energy. But I was too young in my faith, too eager to see a conversion to recognize the counterfeit.

"I just want to give you a hug," he said.

"Cool, man." I stood up thinking it would be a bro hug, three pats on the back.

Instead, he came in with a full frontal bear hug, pressing every inch of his body against mine. His crotch pressed against mine—that's how close he was. He squeezed me, put his head on my left shoulder, and let out this breath: "Ahhhh."

Weird, but okay. This guy just accepted Christ. He struck me as weird to begin with, and weird people do weird things.

We sat back down and kept talking. Then it happened again. He stood up, started shaking: "I feel this energy rushing through my body." Another hug request. Same exact thing—head on my shoulder, that exhale.

By the second time, I was thinking: *Okay, this is getting weird.* But I let it happen.

THE BOOKS AND THE CONFESSION

After the second hug, we sat back down. That's when he stood up and walked to that bookshelf God had warned me about. He pulled out several books—two or three—with satanic imagery on the covers. It was the first time in my life I'd been in the presence of satanic literature.

He put them on the table. "I want you to take these out of my house for me."

I took my Bible and set it on top of his books—a power move, looking back—and said, "I'll take them out of your house and burn them."

He was standing over me to my right, and suddenly he screamed angrily: "NO!"

"All right," I said, "but you don't need to yell at me."

He backed up. "I just don't like people burning books."

We sat back down, and that's when he dropped the bomb.

"Hey, I got to tell you something."

"What's that?"

"I'm a member of the Church of Satan."

My brain scrambled to make sense of it. I thought: *Okay, yeah, that's what God was warning me about. Strong spiritual warfare. This dude used to be a member of the Church of Satan, but praise God, he's saved by grace now.*

Jesus said, *"No one can serve two masters, for either he will hate the one and love the other, or he will be devoted to the one and despise the other..."* (Matthew 6:24 ESV). But I didn't realize he was playing a game, tricking me into thinking he could be saved while holding on to darkness.

Then came the third time. He stood up shaking again: "I feel this energy rushing through my body." Another hug request. Same exact ritual. Head on my shoulder, that exhale. After three hours and three of these encounters, I was exhausted and drained.

Three hugs. Three transfers. And the books as a bridge between them. Looking back, I see the pattern now—a dark trinity, a mockery of conversion. He was using physical contact and ritualistic breathing to transfer something. To take something. To leave something behind. He was mimicking what he thought demonic possession looked like in reverse—playing out his twisted idea of what being "possessed" by the Holy Spirit would look like.

As a satanist, he knew possession from the dark side. He'd probably seen or participated in rituals where people shook and convulsed under demonic influence. So when he needed to fake a conversion, he drew from that playbook. The shaking, the energy, the dramatic physical manifestations—it was all theater. Dark theater.

We wrapped up. Before leaving, I talked to him about coming to church Sunday. "Yeah, I'll be there," he said. I took those books, got in my car, and drove away.

Looking in the rearview mirror at his house, I felt different. Like I'd left a piece of myself there but also had something new with me. Something that wasn't me.

THE THEFT

I called my pastor and asked if I could throw the books in the church dumpster—I didn't want them in my house. He thought it would be fine to take them home to throw them away, but said that if I didn't feel comfortable, I could use the church dumpster. I chose the dumpster.

Jay never came to church. Never returned my emails. When I'd email him weeks later, he finally replied: "I tried it, but the Christian thing didn't work for me." He mentioned some ancient religion he was looking into.

For a year, I refused to believe he hadn't become a Christian. Every time I went to that dock for deliveries, Jay received my freight. We'd make small talk, but the real conversation was gone. I told myself he was just weird, working out his salvation.

But that day I'd left his house, something had been stolen from me.

I used to wake up religiously every morning—not because I had to, but because I wanted to. Two, three hours early sometimes, just eating up God's Word. The Holy Spirit spoke to me so clearly. But the morning after Jay's house, it was different. I sat down to read and felt nothing. A dull day. No connection.

A week passed. A month. It got worse. I started getting angry at God. "Why aren't You talking to me? What did I do?"

One morning, I sat on my couch, closed my Bible, and knew—not said, but knew—tomorrow morning I wouldn't wake up early to do this anymore. And I didn't.

I didn't stop believing. Jesus Christ is my Savior, always has been, always will be. But my dedication to understanding my Maker reached a point where I felt so hopeless because I couldn't hear Him.

THE REVELATION

A year later, I was on lunch break, telling this story to a friend from church, when the Holy Spirit suddenly lit up like a light bulb in my head and connected all the dots.

"He never had any intention of becoming a Christian," the Spirit revealed. "He knew exactly what he was doing. He lured you to his house to release something on you."

Paul wrote about this kind of deception: *"For such persons do not serve our Lord Christ, but their own appetites, and by smooth talk and flattery they deceive the hearts of the naive"* (Romans 16:18 ESV). I had been naive. I had walked into that house on a spiritual high, carrying the fire of evangelism but not the full armor of God.

The rage that hit me in that moment was volcanic. When I became a Christian, my rage and hatred for humanity had disappeared instantly. But after Jay's trap, it started coming back. And when I realized what he'd done, it exploded.

I was going to confront him.

But when I went for my next delivery, for the first time since I'd met him, Jay wasn't there. Next week, not there. Week after week, month after month—he was gone. Other workers would say, "Oh, he's on the other side of the building," or, "He transferred to another department."

I'd seen this guy dozens of times over the years. Now suddenly, right when I figured out what he'd done, he vanished.

THE WEIGHT

What I didn't know then—what would take me years to learn—was that what he brought into my life that day was spiritual oppression. Not the Hollywood possession with levitating chairs. It was a weight: a numbing pressure on my spirit that clouded my intimacy with the Lord.

The prophet Isaiah described something similar: "*We grope for the wall like the blind; we grope like those who have no eyes; we stumble at noon as in the twilight, among those in full vigor we are like dead men*" (Isaiah 59:10 ESV). That was me—stumbling in spiritual twilight.

For years, I lived with it and grew accustomed to it. The oppression became like a constant low-grade cold. It made the Holy Spirit's voice distant, muffled. I told myself I was fine. In truth, I was limping.

I started my podcast during this time. The show helped me understand the darker side of the spiritual world, the warfare they don't teach in church. But I still carried that weight.

THE DELIVERANCE

Years passed. Last August—and here the calendar gives me comfort because satan never gets to steal the specificity of grace—I was attending Alan DiDio's Armed Media conference. After speaking about podcasting, two men approached me.

"Do you ever have spiritual oppression or attacks because of what you do?"

Usually, I'd give the closed-off answer: "No, God's got me." But that day I was raw. "Yeah, I got two witches coming after me right now"—that's a whole other story for later.

One stepped aside. "This is my friend Rob, a deliverance minister. He wants to pray for you."

Rob said, "I want to pray a prayer of impartation on you—that you would have eyes to see and ears to hear the attack before it comes."

My hands were in my pockets—I'm timid in public. He told me, "Take your hands out of your pockets and receive this."

My palms got warm. I physically felt it—a spiritual weight lifted off me.

That evening, I realized: I feel good. I haven't felt this good since before I went to Jay's house.

THE LESSON

Jesus gave His disciples authority over unclean spirits: *"Behold, I have given you authority to tread on serpents and scorpions, and over all the power of the enemy, and nothing shall hurt you"* (Luke 10:19 ESV). I had been trying to operate in that authority without complete surrender to God's full calling. The gap in my armor had let the enemy lodge his attack.

That deliverance didn't erase the memory or shame of being tricked. But it restored what had been stolen: my frequency with the Lord.

The thing about spiritual oppression is that it doesn't turn you into a monster. It just makes the edge between clarity and confusion thin. You keep going to church, keep reading your Bible, keep praying, but the Voice that used to speak like a Friend becomes Someone you strain to hear.

My shame was complex. I felt like a fool for being tricked. But the Lord uses even our gullibility. The experience taught me boundaries I didn't know I needed: you can be bold without being reckless. You can be loving and still wise.

James wrote: *"Submit yourselves therefore to God. Resist the devil, and he will flee from you"* (James 4:7 ESV). But I had only done half the equation. I was trying to resist the devil without being fully submitted to God's complete plan for my life. I had accepted salvation, but I was still running from the full calling—the inheritance, the spiritual authority that came with being who God designed me to be.

There are other things I learned: how the enemy uses theatre. Jay wasn't simply confused. He knew the script that would move him through a doorway into my spirit. He knew the choreography to get close enough to take something. Many spiritual attacks aren't dramatic; they're simple manipulations, small exposures meant to introduce a weight that slowly numbs your spiritual hearing.

In the years since, I've learned to be wary without being paranoid. I've learned to rely on a community of saints who will give godly counsel and tell me practical things: don't go down into basements, and when someone's hug feels suffocating, trust the Holy Spirit's discomfort.

Listen: I don't say this to make myself look brave. I'm not. I say it because the story shows how God chooses stubborn people like me to be part of His larger tapestry. I was a trucker who didn't know what to do with spiritual darkness. But the Lord used my ignorance and willingness, my new zeal and simple prayer, to teach me something crucial: salvation is free, but walking in spiritual authority requires complete surrender to God's full calling.

The Lord's kindness isn't always loud. Sometimes it's a warm palm on your own, a prayer that offers deliverance, a Voice that says, "You were targeted, but I have not left you." That's the sentence that kept me from becoming bitter.

And it's the sentence that prepared me for what was coming next, because God wasn't done with me. The calling was still there. And now I had learned, the hard way, that I can't do God's work in my own strength.

You need His full armor. You need to accept not just salvation, but the inheritance—all of it, even the parts that scare you. Take your hands out of your pockets when someone offers to pray. You never know when a simple act of faith will reconnect you to the Voice you thought you had lost.

5
The Voice on Germantown Pike

I would be lying if I said that the encounter with the satanist at his house didn't terrify me.

It did. And it left scars that lasted for years. The oppression, the heaviness, the lingering fear—it didn't just vanish overnight. That day etched itself into my soul. It taught me what spiritual warfare really looked like when it came knocking on my own doorstep.

But to understand how I got from that dark place to standing on a conference stage years later, finally receiving deliverance, I'm going to take you back to me sitting behind the wheel of a tractor trailer. I need to tell you about what happened in between—how God called me to start *The Confessionals* while I was still carrying that spiritual weight, driving a truck, unable to hear His voice clearly.

Here's what I can tell you with absolute certainty: no matter how many days, weeks, or months I wrestled with the fallout from Jay's house, no matter how many years I walked through seasons of spiritual dryness, I never once doubted who Jesus

Christ was. I never questioned my faith. I never considered walking away. Why? Because I had already encountered Him in a real and authentic way. And once you truly encounter Christ, once you have tasted and seen that He is real, there is no going back.

When you know who the Lord is, you don't have to understand every detail about your situation or the circumstances pressing in around you. You don't have to have all the answers. All you need to know is that He is real, that He is present, and that He is still at work today. If you can hold on to that truth, then your faith doesn't collapse when life gets hard. You don't have to scramble for explanations when storms hit. You endure, you cling to Him, and you trust that His will is greater than your own.

That was how I kept moving forward after Jay's trap. I weathered the storm and prayed for the best, knowing that the best always aligned with God's will.

So I kept on trucking. Literally, this was still years before that conference, years before the deliverance. I was driving my rig, trying to stay joyful even though the oppression made everything feel muffled and distant. My marriage with Lindsay was strong, and I truly believed God had given me trucking as the next great thing in my life. I used to joke that I had the trifecta—Jesus, Lindsay, and trucking.

I thought I was content with that. But day after day, mile after mile, looking out the windshield at the world passing by, it started to wear on me. And deep down, I knew the truth that I was made for something more. That reality started gnawing at me on the inside.

The thing is, I had attended Bible college because I felt called to ministry during my high school years. I knew the

Lord had put the call of evangelism on my life. Maybe He was preparing me for something I couldn't yet understand. But in college, I chased everything but that. I tried pastoral ministry. I tried youth ministry. I even tried business. And in the end, I didn't graduate. I never once pursued evangelism the way I was called to.

So there I was—driving a truck, staring through the glass at the road ahead, feeling the weight of the world passing me by. I loved Jesus, I loved Lindsay, and I loved trucking. But that emptiness started to creep in. I knew there had to be more, but I wanted to be the one to decide what that "more" was. Perhaps I'd start a business or return to school. Maybe I'd get into real estate or coaching or who knows what. I had no specific plan, but I wanted to be the architect of whatever came next. I wanted to pick my own adventure.

Most of my days in the truck I filled with sermons. I had the speakers turned up, letting the voices of pastors and preachers pour into me. I wanted to learn as much as I could. I wanted to saturate myself in truth. The more I listened, the more that fire inside me—the evangelistic side of me—started to wake up again.

But in my mind, that particular ship had sailed, and the calling had passed me by. I convinced myself I had missed it. One day, I figured, I'd have kids, and they would be my ministry. I'd find something else to pour myself into—something I chose. I told myself that was enough. And in some ways, it was. I was involved in my local church, a small but growing body of believers. I was happy to pitch in wherever help was needed. And if that had been the only thing God asked of me, I would have done it. I think He would have been pleased with that too—but only if that was the full extent of His calling on my life.

The truth was, He was stirring something deeper. He had called me to more, and now that my heart belonged to Him fully, He was waking that calling again.

THE VOICE ON GERMANTOWN PIKE

I can still see the exact spot where I was driving when it happened. It's burned into my memory like a photograph.

I was driving down Germantown Pike in my truck. The sun was out. The day was clear. But I wasn't in the best mood, because I hated going into the city. Philadelphia was ahead of me, and driving a big truck into tight streets filled me with a low buzz of anxiety every time. It felt like disaster could strike at any moment. One wrong move, one bad turn, and it could all go south. That stress weighed heavily, and over the years, it added up. It felt like it was aging me faster.

As I focused on the road that day, I had a seemingly rare moment when the Holy Spirit broke through the spiritual fog I was living in and spoke to me. Though I wasn't hearing the Holy Spirit with the consistency I had before Jay's house, I did start hearing the voice of the Holy Spirit again.

By then, I had plenty of experience with His voice, and I had learned how He spoke to me from the hours of morning devotions and prayer all day in the truck. I had learned His language. Jesus said it plainly: *"My sheep hear my voice, and I know them, and they follow me"* (John 10:27 ESV). I was finally learning what it meant to be one of His sheep.

I remember my son asking me last year how to hear the Holy Spirit. He was in first grade at the time, and we were driving to school. It was around seven in the morning when he asked me, "Daddy, how do you hear the Holy Spirit?" Talk about a deep question for a first grader.

But my boy has the heart of an evangelist. He carries it just like I do.

So I told him a story. I reminded him of the day we brought his little sister home from the hospital. He was almost three years old, and he got to hold her on the couch. I watched him cradle her tiny body, talking to her softly, telling her how much he loved her. I asked him if he thought she understood what he was saying at the time. He said no.

And he was right. She didn't understand him. She was brand-new to this world. She didn't know our language. However, as time passed, she began to pick it up. When we said his name, she would turn her head toward him. When we said food, she would see something go into her mouth. Little by little, she learned by being in our environment with us.

I told my son that's how it works with the Holy Spirit. If you want to learn His voice, you have to spend time with Him. You have to pray. You have to listen. You have to put yourself in the Holy Spirit's environment. The more time you spend, the more familiar you become with His language and how He speaks to you. Eventually, you don't just hear Him—you recognize His voice.

I learned the Lord's voice one year around Easter. I was driving and felt a strong, overwhelming urge to invite my boss to church. It was so clear, I almost pulled over. However, I then thought about it logically and convinced myself it was ridiculous. He was my boss. What if he said no? That would be awkward. What if he said yes and actually came? That might be even worse. What if he walked into my Pentecostal church and turned out to be a Calvinist or something? The whole thing felt like a disaster waiting to happen, so I didn't do it. I kept my mouth shut.

The week after Easter, I was talking to another driver who was a Christian. In passing, he mentioned that our boss had been looking for a new church for his family. It hit me like a ton of bricks. Time froze in that moment. I realized I had missed it. I had heard the Holy Spirit clearly, and I had ignored Him. The Scripture rang in my head: *"Whoever knows the right thing to do and fails to do it, for him it is sin"* (James 4:17 ESV).

We often pretend God's calling and direction is a choice on our part or a suggestion on His part. But, in reality, it is a command, and if we don't do it, we are out of order. That was when I really learned: when that overwhelming sense hits me, when that inner voice speaks, I can't debate it. I can't second-guess it. I have to act.

That was how I learned the language of my Father.

And that's what I was doing in my truck day after day, sermon after sermon—learning His heavenly language.

So there I was, driving down Germantown Pike, heading into the city with that usual weight of anxiety pressing on me. I don't think I was even praying at the time. I might have had a sermon on, or maybe it was sports talk radio—honestly, I don't remember. What I do remember is the moment the Lord spoke.

It wasn't subtle. It wasn't something I had to decipher. It hit me like a freight train.

The Holy Spirit said, clear as day: "You're going to start a podcast, and you're going to work with a man named Wes Germer from *Sasquatch Chronicles.*"

I gripped the wheel tighter. My stomach dropped. I knew exactly who He was talking about.

THE CALL

I had been listening to Wes for years. His show was all about people sharing their encounters with Bigfoot. And for a guy like me—who had grown up fascinated by the unknown, who would spend mornings watching MonsterQuest on the History Channel before heading out to work—a show like that hooked me right away.

I still remember the first time I stumbled onto it. I didn't even know what a podcast was back then. I had just typed "Bigfoot radio" into Google, hoping something would pop up, and that's how I found *Sasquatch Chronicles*. I didn't know how to use a podcast app, so I'd just go straight to the website and listen from there. This was around 2015, before podcasts were mainstream.

So when God told me I was going to start one—and not just start one, but work with Wes himself—I knew exactly what He meant. And I didn't want it.

Podcasting? That wasn't even on my radar. It wasn't in the realm of possibilities I'd been considering for my life. I'd been dreaming about doing something more, sure, but I wanted to be the one picking what that something was. I didn't know exactly, but I wanted to choose. Podcasting felt like God was hijacking my plans before I even made them.

My life was simple right then—Jesus, Lindsay, trucking. And while I knew I wanted more eventually, I wanted it on my terms, in my timing. The last thing I wanted was God complicating it with something I'd never even considered. But at the same time, something in me yielded. I knew the voice of God when I heard it. I knew better than to fight it. If He was saying this, then it was going to happen.

Still, I made a deal with myself right there in the truck. I wasn't going to seek it out. I wasn't going to force it. If the Lord wanted this podcast to happen, He would have to open every door Himself. Like Gideon with his fleece, I was putting it all in God's hands to make it happen.

That night when I returned home, I told Lindsay. I laid out the whole thing—what God had spoken, what it meant, how I didn't want it but knew it would happen. I told her she would be my witness. When the pieces started falling into place, I wanted her to remember this conversation. She tucked it away in her mind, the same way I did, and we just went on with life.

The next day, I went back to work like nothing had changed. I kept driving. I kept hauling freight. But deep down, I knew something had shifted.

About a month later, I was backing my truck into the dock late one night. It was around 8:30, the sky was dark, and I was getting ready to head home. That's when my phone buzzed. Facebook Messenger was ringing.

I looked down, and the name on the screen stopped me cold.

Wes Germer.

From *Sasquatch Chronicles*.

I froze. My heart pounded. I hadn't reached out to him. I had never messaged him. I had never tried to make contact. And yet, here he was, calling me directly.

I sat in that truck staring at the screen, and I knew exactly what was happening. God's words from Germantown Pike were unfolding before my eyes. It reminded me of Isaiah 30:21 (ESV): *"And your ears shall hear a word behind you, saying, 'This is the way, walk in it....'"* God had shown me the way, and now He was opening the door.

I answered the call, still in shock.

On the other end of the line, Wes introduced himself. His voice was calm, familiar, the same voice I had been listening to through his podcast for years. He asked if I had ever been on his show before to share a Bigfoot encounter.

I told him no. I didn't have a Bigfoot encounter to share. I was just fascinated by the topic. I loved hearing other people's stories, but I didn't have one of my own.

There was a short pause, and then Wes just said, "Oh, okay," and moved on. It wasn't a big deal to him, but for me, that call meant everything.

We ended up talking for a while about different things. Honestly, I don't remember most of what we said. I was too caught up in the weight of the moment. All I could think about was the day on Germantown Pike, when God had spoken so clearly. I could feel His hand all over this.

And then, toward the end of the call, Wes said something that sealed it. Almost casually, he said, "You know, I think you'd be a good podcaster."

The words hit me like a hammer.

A month earlier, God had told me this exact thing—that I would start a podcast and work with Wes Germer from *Sasquatch Chronicles*. And now, out of nowhere, here was Wes himself, speaking that same calling back to me.

In that moment, I knew the clock had started. The calling was in motion.

BUILDING IN THE DARK

I hung up the phone, sat in silence in my truck, and thought about what had just happened. God had spoken, and then He had confirmed it. There was no getting around it.

Sometimes I wonder what would have happened if I had argued with God back then. What if I had said no? Would He have passed the assignment to someone else? Or would He have doubled down, like He did with Pharaoh, bending me until I obeyed? I don't know the answer to that. But I do know that after that call, I didn't resist. I accepted it.

I didn't have a microphone set up. I didn't know how to record. I hadn't even thought about what the show would be called. But deep down, I knew it had already begun.

That night, I went home and told Lindsay about the call. I told her everything that Wes had said. I told her how it lined up with what God had spoken to me weeks earlier. She looked at me, nodded, and reminded me that she was my witness. The Lord had made it clear.

From that point forward, I was a podcaster—even though I hadn't recorded a single episode yet.

After that call with Wes, I knew the path was set. But knowing it and stepping into it were two very different things. I had no idea how to actually do what God was calling me to. I didn't know the first thing about recording a podcast.

So I went back to the basics.

I dug out my old equipment—a beat-up M-Audio Nova microphone, an audio interface that I hadn't touched in years. I had to relearn how to connect it all to the computer and make it work. And even then, I was staring at the next big question: once I record something, where do I even put it? How do people find it?

These were things that are almost laughably easy now. But back in January of 2017, podcasting wasn't as streamlined. The tools were clunky. The process wasn't laid out step by step. You had to figure it out on your own. So that's what I did. I spent night after night, after long days in the truck, researching, tinkering, testing, trying to piece it all together.

At the same time, I started thinking about what the show would even be called. I hadn't been given any specific direction from the Lord other than: podcast, and work with Wes Germer. That was it. So I had to start shaping its identity myself.

Naturally, I thought about Wes's advice. After our first few conversations, one of the things he told me was not to box myself in. "Don't name your show something that's going to trap you," he said. "Leave it open so you can grow with it." That stuck with me.

So I started asking myself: what exactly would this show be? If I were going to interview people like Wes did, what would I be asking them about? What kind of stories would they be sharing with me?

And then it clicked.

I pictured someone coming to me with an experience they had never told anyone before—something strange, something supernatural, something they were afraid to speak out loud. I pictured them sitting down and unburdening themselves, almost like someone entering a booth to confess. They weren't talking to a priest, but they were confessing nonetheless. And I was the one sitting on the other side of the screen, listening.

That's when the name came to me. *The Confessionals.*

That was what people were doing. They were confessing. They were finally sharing the thing they had held back from everyone else. And I would be there to hear it, to hold it, and to share it with the world.

Once the name settled in my spirit, I knew it was right.

From there, the logistics took over. I had to figure out how to record virtual conversations, which at that point was a headache. I had to test different software, different setups. I had to learn how to edit audio well enough that people would actually listen. It was hours of trial and error.

And I did all of this while driving a truck 12 hours a day, sometimes 14. I would get home exhausted, eat dinner quickly, and then disappear into the third bedroom of our house to work on this podcast that didn't exist yet. Eyes burning, surviving on three hours of sleep a night, just grinding.

It was brutal. But I knew what I was building toward. Paul's words kept me going: *"Let us not grow weary of doing good, for in due season we will reap, if we do not give up"* (Galatians 6:9 ESV). I was sowing in exhaustion, believing for a harvest I couldn't yet see.

Finally, on January 19, 2017, I hit publish. *The Confessionals* was live.

Episode 1: "Farmer Sees Two Sasquatch."

That first episode was easy in one sense, because I had already been talking to the farmer for months. He lived in western Pennsylvania and had seen two Bigfoot on his property. At one point, he even had one in his scope. He could have pulled the trigger but didn't. That was the story that opened the door.

The following week, Episode 2 went up. A man who had an extremely close encounter with a UFO.

Episode 3 was Lindsay. My wife came on and shared her encounters with the hat man—something I didn't even know she had experienced until we started talking about the show. She became my first in-studio guest.

Episode 4 was a professor I had back in college, the one who used to talk about the Nephilim and sounded crazy to most people. I thought he might sound crazy to me too, but the more I listened, the more I realized he was onto something.

So right out of the gate, in my first month, I had four episodes: Bigfoot, UFOs, the hat man, and the Nephilim. Four topics. Four different worlds.

And just like that, *The Confessionals* was running.

THE WEIGHT OF THE CALLING

I had no idea what I had just stepped into. At the time, I thought *The Confessionals* was just about stories. I thought it was about giving people a platform to talk about the things they couldn't share anywhere else. I didn't see the bigger picture. I didn't understand the spiritual weight of it.

Looking back, I realize I was stepping into a battle I wasn't prepared for. Again, as Paul warned: *"For we do not wrestle against flesh and blood, but against the rulers, against the authorities, against the cosmic powers over this present darkness..."* (Ephesians 6:12 ESV). Every story that would come through my show—whether Bigfoot or UFO or shadow person—was touching that cosmic battle. But at the time, all I knew was that God had called me, and I was going to obey.

So I threw myself into it.

I treated *The Confessionals* like it was my full-time job, even though it didn't pay me a dime. In fact, it cost me money. But I gave it everything I had.

My days started early behind the wheel of the truck, then I'd come home, wolf down dinner, and head into my studio. Night after night, teaching myself how to edit, producing episodes, working on every detail.

This pace went on for nearly two and a half years. Truck all day, podcast all night. Rinse, repeat.

Most people would have burned out. But I knew God had placed this calling on me.

For the first ten months, I released an episode each week without fail. Rain or shine, exhausted or not, the show went out. And little by little, people started listening.

By October 2017, something else started to happen. The news cycle began whispering about UFOs. Or as they started calling them, UAPs (Unidentified Aerial Phenomena). The government was dropping hints. Leaks were surfacing. For the first time, it wasn't just fringe researchers talking about it—it was coming from official channels.

At first, I didn't care. To me, it was background noise. I was still "Bigfoot Tony." I was still grinding away, focused on cryptids and hauntings and shadow people. Government UFO talk didn't register with me as significant. I thought, *That's cool, I guess,* and moved on.

But I had no idea how much that moment was going to matter in the years ahead. I didn't see how it would shape the conversations I'd have, the guests who would come on my show, and the way my own understanding of the supernatural would expand.

At the time, all I knew was that I was being obedient. I thought I was just recording strange stories. I had no clue that what I was doing was about to collide head-on with spiritual warfare in ways I never imagined.

And then Charlie called.

A soldier.

With a story about a secret mission.

And a downed aircraft that did not come from earth.

6
Language of the Fallen

Now the whole earth had one language and the same words. ...And the Lord said, "Behold, they are one people, and they have all one language, and this is only the beginning of what they will do. And nothing that they propose to do will now be impossible for them."

—Genesis 11:1,6 ESV

THE INTERVIEW THAT CHANGED EVERYTHING

Two years had passed since I'd launched *The Confessionals.* Hundreds of interviews. Countless stories of Bigfoot, UFOs, shadow people, and things that shouldn't exist. Each one adding another piece to a puzzle I was only beginning to understand. But nothing had prepared me for Charlie.

In 2019, I interviewed a man named "Charlie." Charlie was an alias as he did not want his real name revealed. We had planned on recording his story months prior, but he got cold feet. So when we connected to finally record his experience, we brainstormed about what to call him so we wouldn't mistakenly say his real name. That's when the idea came in, simply of Alpha, Bravo, "Charlie." So, Charlie it was, and with hindsight on knowing how his experience would pan out, I almost feel like Charlie is his real name, and never greeted him afterward by any other name.

In a sense, this interview was like any other interview at the time. Raw, intense, and mysterious. The kind of story that makes you lean forward in your chair. But what I didn't realize then was that this conversation would become one of the cornerstone moments of my understanding of the supernatural realm.

At the time, I didn't fully grasp what Charlie had been part of. I didn't fully see the spiritual warfare woven into every page of his story. But as the years went on, and I began to dig and learn more about spiritual warfare, the second heaven, and the reality behind so-called "aliens," I kept coming back to this interview. Charlie's words started connecting dots that I didn't even know needed to be connected. I don't think Charlie totally understood how deep and impactful his experience was and what keys it held to understanding the supernatural realm. If understanding the supernatural realm was a 1,000-piece puzzle, Charlie's experience holds about a dozen pieces alone.

This wasn't just a UFO story. It was a spiritual intelligence leak.

THE SOLDIER'S PATH

Charlie was ex-military. Though "ex" feels like a technicality in his case. He didn't just serve in his government's armed forces and decide to retire when he had had his fill. He was absorbed into something deeper, stranger, and more compartmentalized than even the military likes to admit. It was so impactful and transformative for Charlie that he went from being an enthusiastic soldier who was looking to excel in his job to counting down the days that his contracted service would expire and he could get out and dodge. And that is exactly what he did too.

What you are about to read was so exponentially impactful on Charlie that he didn't just take the opportunity to get out of the service at the first chance; he left the country and set up a new life somewhere else that was far away from anyone or anything related to this incident.

Charlie was top of his class in intelligence training. One of the best performers. Second-highest overall. He got to choose his orders, or at least, that's how it was presented to him as to how it was to work. He picked his assignment and got the soft confirmation that assured him it was in the works, and he was told to wait on base until his orders were finalized. And then, nothing.

As he waited, he saw everyone else being shipped out. It seemed like he was last in line as if he were one of the worst in his graduating class, and he was being left behind. He waited for weeks, and then weeks turned into months with no answers. He was being given just busywork while the rest of his class had moved on.

Then one day, without warning, a new set of orders showed up that was a different assignment from the one he had chosen. It was a different location with no explanation or heads-up. Just a sealed packet and 24 hours to get on a plane. Though he asked questions, Charlie got nothing but shrugs and one sentence that stuck with him. "It came from above." Charlie didn't think much of it at the time as he had seen the kind of bureaucracy that comes with many forms of government, and the military was certainly no different.

Charlie was trained for an intelligence role, but not specifically for the tasks he would be handling. Once he arrived at his new post, which was a highly secure underground facility, he had to go through an additional 8 to 12 weeks of intense training specific to his assignment.

With this background being laid out, I have to interject here to say that there was something else going on here. An unknown entity was redirecting Charlie, using the word "entity" very loosely. Sure on the surface it looked like military, but this was something higher. He was pulled off one path he wanted and placed on another, and not by accident. This was not due to an administrative error; it was intentional.

I've come to believe that the spiritual and physical realms don't run on their own timeliness independently from one another; they lock together. What looks like a "glitch" in the system is often divine or demonic timing and strategy. What feels like a mistake might actually be positioning for the future, and I think Charlie was placed, not passed over.

THE MISSION

Something was moving and operating in the background of Charlie's life, opening and closing doors. Whatever that something was, it slammed this door shut and then opened another one. Behind it was a mission that even his commanding officers didn't fully understand. Or if they did, they weren't going to be offering their interpretations anytime soon. It was a recovery job of a downed aircraft. This was nothing out of the ordinary for someone in his field until the details started leaking in.

He and a team of eight soldiers, along with a crew of **eight civilian** scientists (high-value assets, as Charlie called them), boarded a scientific research vessel flagged to another country. No one knew what they were actually looking for because the instructions were very vague, but the urgency was high. The secrecy was beyond anything he'd experienced in any previous missions, as this was his fourth now. The objective was clear: locate a downed aircraft, extract any data, and destroy it with thermite. There was no ISO prep conducted, which was a big red flag, as it was a major break in protocol, because this was used for ID in case someone was captured.

The journey to the downed aircraft consisted of a 36-hour boat ride and a two-day hike to location. This was not an afternoon hike that would be quick and relatively painless. As the ship reached about two nautical miles off the coast of the target area, Charlie, joined by a team of eight military personnel and a group of civilian scientists, set off to the shore on two RHIBs (Rigid-Hulled Inflatable Boats).

He described the area they were in as cold, wooded, and hostile territory. The team moved covertly, and that meant all ship communications were cut to maintain operational secrecy. The terrain they were covering was described as rocky and wooded with no snow, but cold enough to be pretty uncomfortable. The team formed a column to isolate the civilians in the middle. Four men up front, scientists in the middle, four men in the rear, which included Charlie.

WHEN COMMUNICATION FAILED

They had preplanned comms check windows to establish their status back to the ship, but during the second window, their radios failed completely, even with high-frequency gear. Charlie and the team couldn't contact the ship or each other beyond a short range. It was as if the environment they entered was not the environment they stayed in. Something changed. Their gear was performing in a way that seemed like there was something interfering with it and blocking them from open communication. Something had shifted, and it wasn't the distance they had traveled. It's as if they entered a steel building where their radio frequencies were being stopped at a wall.

Two recon scouts from the team went ahead to try to reach higher ground in hopes of better communication. They were gone for the entire night, leaving the camp they had left behind to hunker down and camp the night out. During that night, internal comms, which were the close-range radios, also began malfunctioning. Weird squawking came through the radios, but no intelligible voices. It was like something was hijacking their gear. Like the territory itself was interfering with their ability to stay connected. Or maybe even worse, they weren't alone. Charlie emphasized that it wasn't interference like they were used to.

It didn't sound like signal bleed or natural frequency disruption. It had a character to it—a sound that felt intentional, not random. The word he used was "squawking"—like a mechanical bird or distorted audio trying to form something, but not quite human. No speech patterns, no language. Just noise. But loud enough to notice, and persistent enough to unsettle the team.

The scientists were nervous. Radios were unreliable. Gear malfunctioned in ways that hinted at interference from something more than terrain or tech.

THE DISCOVERY

When they arrived at the crash site, the weirdness came out of the shadows and stood in full daylight. The aircraft they found wasn't just unconventional. It didn't make sense. It wasn't burned out or wrecked in any traditional way. It had power. It had structure. And it had no signs of human origin. Matte black checkerboard surface, eerily cold ceramic tiles, and no insignias or markings of any known military force. No tail numbers. No flags. No visible propulsion systems. Somehow, the onboard systems were still running.

That alone is enough to raise eyebrows. But what sealed it for me, and what has never left me since, was what Charlie found inside.

He was tasked with extracting data from the onboard computers. Nothing new. But when he got to one particular terminal, he saw characters on the screen that froze him in place. They weren't English. Not Russian. Not Arabic, Chinese, Korean, or anything else he was trained to identify. And Charlie was trained to visually recognize at least seven languages on sight. This language wasn't just foreign. It was something else entirely.

He tried flipping through his field manual to match it to anything known. That's when one of the scientists stepped up beside him and said something that still sends chills down my spine.

"You're not going to find it in there," the man said.

Charlie looked up, puzzled.

The man's face was tense. His chin quivering like someone wrestling with whether or not to speak a truth they weren't supposed to.

"It's Enochian," the man said quietly.

THE FORBIDDEN LANGUAGE

Charlie didn't know what that meant. Neither did I, when I first heard it. But I know now.

Enochian is the name of a language allegedly given to humanity through occult practices. A so-called "angelic" language communicated by spirits to men like John Dee and Edward Kelley in the 1500s. But let's not sanitize the word "angelic." These were not angels in white robes and halos. These were fallen spirits, masquerading as divine messengers. Just like satan has always done.

The scientist called it what it was. "An ancient demon language."

When Charlie told me that, I felt something shift. This wasn't about alien technology. This was about forbidden knowledge. The same kind the book of Enoch describes—knowledge the watchers gave to mankind before the flood. Knowledge that corrupted humanity so deeply that God had to wash the world clean. As it says in Genesis 6:5 (ESV), *"The Lord saw that the wickedness of man was great in the earth, and that every intention of the thoughts of his heart was only evil continually."*

This aircraft wasn't just flying through airspace. It was trespassing from another realm. And the language inside it? That was the signature. The calling card. The proof of who was really behind it.

Think about what this means. If these "aliens" are using a language that occultists claim came from fallen angels, then we're not dealing with visitors from another planet. We're dealing with the same entities that have been deceiving humanity since Eden. The same ones Jesus warned about when He said, *"For false christs and false prophets will arise and perform great signs and wonders, so as to lead astray, if possible, even the elect"* (Matthew 24:24 ESV).

The scientist didn't explain himself. He just said, "Get your job done, and let's get out of here."

So Charlie got to work. Plugged in, extracted what he could, wiped the systems. Same procedures he'd done a hundred times. But this time, something was different. The longer he stayed inside the craft, the more he felt the environment turning in on itself. The lights were still on, the gear still worked, but everything else felt like it was pulsing under the surface.

Like the place had a heartbeat.

Charlie didn't call it that. But the way he described it, that's what I kept thinking. Something about the craft felt aware. Not just advanced, not just powerful, but conscious. Like it had its own presence. And that presence wasn't passive.

THE JOURNEY BACK

After the data pull, they laid thermite strips across the hardware, then rigged a delayed EMP (Electromagnetic Pulse, burst of radiation that disrupts or damages electronic equipment) to make sure nothing usable survived. Charlie stepped outside, and for the first time since entering the ship, he could finally breathe again. But the pressure never really left.

They packed up. The sun was already coming up. The hike back to the shore would take two days. That should have been the easy part.

Instead, it's where things started unraveling.

The first signs were subtle. Static on the radios. Comms squelching with no voices. Then it got worse. The internal comms stopped working altogether. The gear malfunctioned without explanation. Batteries that had held power the day before went dead. Thermal scopes flickered. It was like something was interfering with the physical environment around them, but no one could pinpoint what or why.

Charlie and his team had seen tech fail in the field before. Terrain can do that. So can elevation. But this was different. This felt like the rules were bending. Like the environment they were in was not behaving like normal terrain.

And here's where I started wondering.

Charlie never used these words, but the more I listened, the more I couldn't shake it. What if they didn't just find a craft? What if they crossed into something?

I have seen this pattern before. People stepping into places that seem normal at first, only to realize later they aren't on the same ground they started on. Portals that don't announce themselves. Spiritual boundaries that don't look like boundaries at all. You walk through a tree line, and suddenly, you are in something else. Another realm.

Like the "Upside Down" in *Stranger Things* on Netflix. But real.

That's what this part of Charlie's story started to sound like. Like they had walked into a different version of the world. One layered over the top of ours. Close enough to look familiar, but just far enough to be dangerous.

THE NIGHT WATCH

They made camp that night along a ridge. Four soldiers on the front line. Four in the back. Scientists staggered out between them. Charlie and his crew held rear overwatch. Standard posture for a dangerous zone. But this didn't feel like standard danger.

He said the woods went too quiet. No bugs. No birds. Just stillness. Like the trees themselves were holding their breath.

They rotated sleep cycles. Two down, two awake. Charlie dozed off with one earbud in, an old Mobb Deep track playing low enough to keep his brain from locking up. Just enough noise to stay half alert. You don't ever fully sleep in the field. Not if you want to wake up.

Then he heard it. His teammate's voice. Sharp, quiet, serious.

"Multiple tangos."

Charlie sat up fast. Pulled the bud out. Slid into prone. Raised his optics. Nothing.

Night vision showed only static and shadows. No movement.

Then he flipped his optics to FLIR (Forward-Looking Infrared).

And that is when everything changed.

THE ORANGE-EYED WATCHERS

When Charlie flipped to FLIR, everything lit up.

Twenty figures. Maybe more. Moving through the trees. No heat signatures, but clear shapes. Humanoid. Upright. Shadow-black with burning orange eyes. Not glowing in the normal sense. These weren't reflections. These weren't goggles. These were eyes that looked back.

He said it chilled him immediately. Not the kind of fear you feel in your body. The kind you feel in your spirit. Like your soul just got noticed.

These weren't extraterrestrials. These were what the Bible calls "principalities and powers." The entities Paul warned us about in Ephesians 6:12 (ESV): *"For we do not wrestle against flesh and blood, but against the rulers, against the authorities, against the cosmic powers over this present darkness…."*

The Enochian text in that craft connected everything. It showed their hand. These beings weren't hiding their identity—they were flaunting it. Using their ancient language, the same one they've been teaching to occultists for centuries, whenever someone opens the door through ritual and rebellion.

These things moved wrong. That's how Charlie described it. Not rushed, not mechanical. Just wrong. Asymmetrical. Off-balance, but still deliberate. Some were tall. Others short. No uniforms. No gear. Just silhouettes gliding through the forest, side to side, weaving between trees like they were part of them.

They didn't come from behind. They came from the direction of the crash site.

And they were headed straight for the front group.

Charlie's team was in overwatch, up on the ridge, watching from a distance. They tried to warn the guys up front using infrared signals—no comms. Just light pulses in the dark, unseen by the human eye. They lassoed the unknowns with FLIR lasers, trying to show their position, but there was no response. The front team never signaled back.

The figures didn't seem to notice them either. Not yet.

Charlie said they just kept moving. Quiet. Focused. Like they had a destination. Or maybe a target.

THE MORNING FIREFIGHT

This is where the story starts bending.

Nothing happened immediately. The figures passed through, and the forest settled. No engagement. No contact.

The guys on Charlie's team were tense but ready. They took turns sleeping. The scientists were rattled, but trying to stay calm. The rest of the night passed in a strange kind of silence. Not peaceful. Just delayed.

But early that morning, it exploded.

Gunfire ripped through the woods.

Sharp. Controlled. M4 bursts. Not panic fire. Not blind shooting. Someone up front had eyes on something and was putting rounds on target. But no one knew what.

The team in the rear mobilized immediately. Charlie said it was like flipping a switch. Their training took over. No panic. Just movement.

But they couldn't see anything. The ridge line and terrain blocked their view. All they had were the sounds—and the instinct that whatever was happening up there, it wasn't part of the original mission.

The front team fell back, grabbing the scientists as they went. One scientist was injured and couldn't move fast. Charlie and two others stayed behind to evac him. The rest pushed forward toward the extraction point. But when Charlie and his group finally made it to the rendezvous location—the others were gone.

So was the RHIB.

The raft that had brought them in had been launched. Empty mags in the sand. Tracks everywhere. Like whoever left had moved fast and under pressure.

But no bodies. No blood. No signs of casualties. Just absence.

THE REALITY FRACTURE

And here's where it gets weird.

Charlie said they were less than an hour behind. No more than that. But when they reached the beach, they couldn't make contact with the ship. And when they finally did—when the signal broke through and the boat responded—everything felt off.

The ship hadn't moved. It was still dark, in blackout mode. But when they boarded, it was like the crew had no idea what had just happened.

The mission brief the next morning confirmed it.

Charlie and the three guys who stayed behind were told they were being activated for a new op. Recovery. Search and rescue. Another team had gone missing while looking for a downed aircraft. They were going in to find them.

But that made no sense.

They were the team.

The mission they had just completed—the one they had risked their lives on—was being erased right in front of them. Rewritten. Like it hadn't happened yet. Or like it had happened somewhere else.

At the time, I didn't know what to make of that. It just sounded strange. Like a mix-up in the paperwork or a cover story being spun in real time.

But now? Now I'm not so sure.

After the debrief, Charlie said he sat in silence for a long time.

The officer in charge stood there, running through a briefing like they were about to deploy for the first time. Like they hadn't already been to the crash site. Like they hadn't already pulled the data, burned the wreck, and barely made it out.

There was no mention of the EMP. No mention of the injured scientist. No mention of the orange-eyed figures.

Just a clean slate. A pretend mission.

Charlie looked around the room. Most of the guys nodded along like everything made sense. But a few of them—the ones who stayed behind with him, the ones who had seen what he saw—their faces didn't match the tone of the room. Their eyes were locked in the same stunned silence.

They weren't hearing this as a briefing. They were hearing it as a rewrite.

TIME STOPS ON THE SHIP

Charlie said he almost spoke up. Almost said something to call it out. But the moment passed. And deep down, he wasn't even sure who he'd be speaking to anymore. He told me it felt like they were living two different versions of the same story.

Later that night, things got worse.

Charlie took a security shift and went to do a sweep of the ship. Nothing unusual. Just making rounds. He made his way to the bridge and stepped inside. It was late. No lights. Just the dim green glow from radar screens and monitors. Everything was quiet.

Too quiet.

He tried to greet the crew on duty. Nothing.

No movement. No response.

He said the men on the bridge were standing perfectly still. Not like they were ignoring him. Like they were frozen. Bodies tilted with the pitch of the ship, but not reacting to it. The whole vessel was rocking with the waves, but these men were locked in place like mannequins.

Charlie stood there for a few seconds, unsure if he was dreaming or losing it. Then he turned and left. Found his teammate—the one he trusted most—brought him back to the bridge.

When they entered together, everything was normal.

The crew looked up. Nodded. Spoke. Like nothing had happened. Like they had been in motion the whole time.

Charlie didn't push it. He didn't even tell them what he had seen. But from that moment on, he started watching the ship differently. It wasn't just the equipment or the silence. It was the people. Some of them started acting like they hadn't even been on the mission. They talked like it hadn't happened. Like it was still ahead of them.

The scientist with the injured hip? Said he got it falling down a ladder during the storm. Nothing about the hike. Nothing about the gunfire.

Charlie couldn't reconcile it. He tried writing things down. Bullet points. Timelines. Cross-checking with the other three guys who had stayed behind. Their notes matched his. Their memories lined up. But everyone else was operating from a different script.

And then it happened again.

Another shift.

This time in the galley. Broad daylight. Charlie walked in and saw a group of people—military and civilian — completely still. Like time had stopped again. Like something had pressed pause, but forgot to tell him. It only lasted a moment. But it was enough.

By now, he had stopped trying to make sense of it.

He wasn't sure if he had experienced something supernatural, or psychological, or something deeper. But when I asked him what he really thought happened, he paused. And then he said something that's stuck with me ever since.

"I'm not even sure if we came back to the same world we left from."

UNDERSTANDING THE PATTERN

At the time, I didn't know what to say to that. I thought he was speaking figuratively. Now I'm not so sure.

Because the more I've learned about this realm—this second heaven, the layer that sits between here and the throne of God—the more I've started to wonder if places like that crash site are more than just coordinates on a map.

What if they're not just openings? What if they're anchor points?

Points of contact between this world and another realm. The second heaven. The place where the fallen operate. The place where the rules bend. Where time slips. Where memory fractures.

The Bible speaks of this in Daniel 10, where an angel tells Daniel he was delayed 21 days by *"the prince of the kingdom of Persia"*—a territorial spirit assigned to that region.

> *Then he continued, "Do not be afraid, Daniel. Since the first day that you set your mind to gain understanding and to humble yourself before your God, your words were heard, and I have come in response to them. But the prince of the Persian kingdom resisted me twenty-one days. Then Michael, one of the chief princes, came to help me, because I was detained there with the king of Persia"* (Daniel 10:12-13 NIV).

These aren't just spiritual battles happening in some abstract realm. They're happening over specific territories, specific coordinates, specific missions. And sometimes, people like Charlie walk right into the middle of them.

What if that ship wasn't just from another place, but another reality? One that intersects with ours. One we can't always see until it's too late. One you can walk into without ever knowing you crossed a line.

I don't think Charlie and his team saw the veil lift. I think they walked right through it. I think they entered something they weren't trained to understand. And when they came back, the damage had already been done.

The Enochian language wasn't just text on a screen. It was a signature. A mark. A message. One that said, they were here.

And once you see that kind of thing, I don't think you ever come all the way back.

THE WARNING

I've replayed this interview more times than I can count. I've sat with Charlie's words in hotel rooms, in editing bays, on long drives with nothing but the sound of his voice cutting through the speakers. And every time, I walk away with the same unsettled feeling.

This wasn't a story. This was a warning. We just didn't know it yet.

Back in 2019, the UFO conversation hadn't gone mainstream. People were still laughing at the idea that aliens could be real. The government hadn't started making disclosures. The world hadn't shifted the way it has now. So when I heard Charlie describe Enochian language on a black craft that radiated cold and pulsed like it was alive, I knew it was strange. But I didn't know it was prophetic.

Now I do.

Now I see the pattern. These ships, these encounters, these fractures in time and memory aren't isolated. They're part of a strategy. A spiritual one. And the entities behind it don't care if we believe in them or not. They've been playing this game a long time. Longer than us. Longer than government. Longer than history books are willing to admit.

And they're not showing up because we've earned their curiosity.

They're showing up because they've been invited. Through ritual. Through rebellion. Through the same kind of forbidden knowledge that corrupted the earth before the flood. The same kind that the book of Enoch says was taught by the watchers to mankind—in exchange for something. There's always an exchange.

Looking back, I believe Charlie and his team were sent to retrieve something that was never meant to be found. Or maybe it was always meant to be found—just not understood. That ship wasn't a discovery. It was a delivery. The language inside it was the clue. The craft may have been the bait.

And the aftermath? The time slips. The memory loss. The fractured accounts and the frozen moments on the ship. Those weren't tech glitches. Those were aftershocks. Spiritual echoes from crossing a line they couldn't see. And once crossed, you don't just walk away untouched.

I think Charlie walked out with more than just his memories.

I think something followed him.

THE ONLY ANSWER

And if this is what we're dealing with—not just machines in the sky, but spiritual warfare wrapped in technology—we need to stop asking what these things are and start asking who.

Because there's a war happening just outside our perception. And every now and then, someone like Charlie stumbles into it, cracks the edge of the curtain, and comes back different.

Most people won't believe him. That's fine.

But I do.

And I believe his story is one more piece of the same truth I've been chasing for years now—the one that always leads back to this: Jesus is the only One who can save us from what's coming.

Because what we're dealing with isn't just deception. It's ancient. It's intelligent. And it's already here.

As Jesus Himself warned: *"And if those days had not been cut short, no human being would be saved. But for the sake of the elect those days will be cut short"* (Matthew 24:22 ESV).

The Enochian language in that craft wasn't just a clue. It was a confession. These entities have been here all along, working through whatever mask serves their purpose—gods, aliens, ascended masters. The names change. The deception remains the same.

And the only protection? The only way through?

The same as it's always been.

Jesus Christ.

Not as an idea. Not as a philosophy. But as Lord and Savior. Because when you're dealing with principalities and powers that can bend time, manipulate memory, and speak languages given by fallen angels, you need more than human strength. You need divine authority.

Charlie learned that the hard way. And his story became one of the most important pieces of evidence I've ever collected—not evidence of aliens, but evidence of the spiritual war we're all part of, whether we know it or not.

THE PATTERN IN THE DARKNESS

Charlie's story haunted me for months after that interview. The Enochian text. The orange-eyed watchers. The way time seemed to fracture and loop on that ship. I kept turning it over in my mind, trying to make sense of entities that could write in the language of fallen angels, that could manipulate reality itself.

But *The Confessionals* doesn't stop. Every week brings new witnesses, new encounters, new pieces of an ever-expanding puzzle. And as the episodes accumulated—now numbering in the hundreds—I began to notice something disturbing. The same patterns that appeared in Charlie's military operation were showing up everywhere.

UFO encounters where beings spoke in ancient languages. Bigfoot sightings where the creatures vanished without using any physical exit. Shadow people that moved through walls. Dogmen that appeared in places they couldn't possibly hide. At first, these seemed like completely different phenomena. Aliens. Cryptids. Interdimensional beings. Demons. We had all these categories, these neat little boxes to sort the impossible into.

But what if the boxes were a deception too? What if these weren't different types of entities at all, but the same fallen beings wearing different costumes for different audiences? Show a military unit something technological. Show a hunter something bestial. Show a child something that matches their nightmares.

Two years after Charlie's interview, I received an email that would drive this truth home with brutal clarity. It came from a man in Eastern Kentucky, and it contained an encounter that shouldn't have been connected to Charlie's story at all. No UFOs. No mysterious text. No military operations.

Just a 15-year-old boy, his grandfather's hunting dogs, and something that walked upright through the Daniel Boone National Forest on two legs.

But as I read his account, I found myself leaning closer to my computer screen, completely absorbed. This wasn't just another cryptid sighting. This was another piece of the same war, the same ancient conflict, just wearing a different face.

The enemy doesn't always come in ships. Sometimes it comes on four legs that rise to two.

7
Dog Versus Dogman

And Jacob was left alone; and there wrestled a man with him until the breaking of the day. And when he saw that he prevailed not against him, he touched the hollow of his thigh; and the hollow of Jacob's thigh was out of joint, as he wrestled with him.

—Genesis 32:24-25 KJV

KYLE'S EMAIL

I get a lot of emails. Hundreds every week, each one containing a piece of someone's story, a fragment of their encounter with the impossible. But Kyle's email stopped me cold.

It was October 2021, and I was sitting in my office, working through the stack of messages that had accumulated over the weekend. Most dogman encounters follow a pattern—a glimpse in the headlights, strange howls in the night, maybe footprints that don't belong to any known animal.

But Kyle's story was different. This wasn't just an encounter. This was a battle.

As I read his account, I found myself leaning closer to my computer screen, completely absorbed. Kyle hadn't just seen a dogman. He'd been hunted by one. And the only reason he was alive to write this email was because his dog—a 120-pound Walker coonhound named Jake—had thrown himself between Kyle and the creature four times, ultimately paying a price that should have killed him.

The way Kyle wrote, with that understated Kentucky directness, made it even more powerful. No embellishment. No dramatics. Just the facts of what happened that night in the Daniel Boone National Forest when he was 15 years old, out hunting raccoons with his grandfather's dogs.

I had to get him on the show.

THE HUNTER'S HERITAGE

When Kyle told his experience on *The Confessionals,* he painted a picture of a world most listeners had never experienced. Eastern Kentucky, in the foothills of the Appalachian Mountains, where subsistence living wasn't a lifestyle choice but a necessity. Where they worked the coal mines or drove hours to a factory job. Where hunting and trapping weren't hobbies, but were how they fed their family and made ends meet.

"I grew up hunting and fishing," Kyle explained, his voice carrying the rhythms of mountain speech. "That's what I was taught to do. That's what I enjoyed doing as a child."

Kyle was raised by his grandparents—Mamaw and Papaw, as they called them in those hills. His grandfather had taught him everything: how to read signs in the forest, how to train a hound from a pup, how to track and trap, how to move through the Daniel Boone National Forest as his people had for generations. This wasn't recreational hunting. This was heritage, passed down father to son, grandfather to grandson, in an unbroken chain stretching back to Daniel Boone himself.

The dogs were central to this life. Kyle's family raised multiple breeds—Black and Tans, Walkers, Redbones, Blueticks, English Mountain Curs, and Feists. Each breed had its purpose, its specialty. But they all shared one thing: they were family.

"We trained every dog with love," Kyle emphasized. "We never beat on them or abused them. They were just as much part of our family as a brother, sister, cousin, or uncle."

This is important to understand. These weren't just hunting tools. They were partners, each with their own personality, their own reputation in the community. In rural Kentucky, a good hunting dog was known by name for counties around. And Old Jake—he was legendary.

THE NIGHT EVERYTHING CHANGED

October 1, 2003. Opening night of coon (raccoon) hunting season in Kentucky. Kyle was 15, eager to get out with the dogs despite his grandfather's failing health. Papaw had heart disease, could barely walk any distance, but he could still drive the truck, still be part of the hunt.

They got a late start that night, and other hunters were already out in the forest. So they drove deeper than usual, six miles down a gravel road that wound into the heart of the Daniel Boone National Forest. No houses. No lights. Just the darkness of the deep woods and whatever moved through them.

Kyle loaded two dogs into the truck's dog box: Bo, a young red tick hound the color of strawberry wine, still learning but showing promise, and Old Jake, the veteran. Jake wasn't just experienced—he was exceptional. At 120 pounds, he was massive for a Walker, built like a small bear with jaws that could crush bone. He'd fought off coyotes multiple times, killed them on the tree when they tried to steal his raccoon. In the community of coon hunters, Jake was famous. When he barked, you could "take that check to the bank and cash it," as Kyle put it. If Jake said there was a raccoon nearby, there was a raccoon nearby.

The hunting process Kyle described was specific, almost ritualistic: They release the dogs and listen. They communicate through their barks—a "locate" when they find a scent trail, long and drawn out like a miniature wolf howl. Then the "bawl bark" as they track, longer than normal barking but shorter than locates. Finally, when the raccoon goes up a tree, they switch to a "chop"—rapid, constant barks that signal they have their prey cornered.

That night started normally. Kyle released the dogs at the end of the road, next to a cliff face. They immediately picked up a scent, working it up the mountain, over the cliff, down the backside. Seven hundred yards from the truck, they treed. Kyle could tell by their barks—Jake's deep, authoritative voice mixed with Bo's younger, eager tones.

His grandfather handed him the .22 rifle. "Better get in there and shoot that raccoon out," he said. At 15, Kyle had done this hundreds of times. Take the gun, the light, the radio, walk in, shoot the raccoon, bring back the dogs. Routine.

But that night, the routine shattered.

WHEN PREDATORS CONVERGE

As Kyle made his way toward the dogs, he heard coyotes in the distance. A big pack, seven or eight by the sound of it. This wasn't unusual—coyotes were common in the Daniel Boone. But these were moving toward the dogs.

"The pack's getting closer," his grandfather radioed. "You need to get in there."

Coyotes will attack dogs, especially when they outnumber them. They hear the barking and think it's an easy meal. Kyle picked up his pace, but before he could reach them, the fight exploded.

He could hear it all clearly—Bo squealing, running, getting away from the pack. But not Jake. Old Jake came off his tree and met them head-on. Kyle could hear the coyotes' death screams as Jake's powerful jaws found their marks. This dog didn't retreat. In his mind, he'd done the work to tree that raccoon, and no pack of coyotes was going to drive him off.

"They're gonna kill him," Kyle's grandfather said over the radio. "You gotta get there."

Kyle was running now, his light bouncing through the trees. The sounds of the battle were terrible—Jake fighting multiple coyotes at once, the squeals and snarls echoing through the hollow. Then suddenly the dynamic changed. It sounded like Bo had returned to help.

Kyle was maybe 50 yards away when his light caught the scene. Jake had a coyote by the throat. The sight of Kyle's light made him release it, and the pack scattered, afraid of the human presence. Kyle went to Jake, checking him over. The big dog was hurt but not badly—some bites, some blood, but he'd held his own against impossible odds.

That should have been the end of it. Kyle should have leashed the dogs and headed back. But behind a massive black oak tree, he heard something that made him think Bo had grabbed one of the coyotes—a wet, choking sound, what Kyle called a "blood gargle."

THE MOMENT REALITY BROKE

Kyle walked around the oak tree, shining his light, expecting to see Bo finishing off a wounded coyote.

What he saw instead changed his life forever.

The thing holding a 40-pound coyote in its mouth wasn't Bo. It wasn't any dog Kyle had ever seen. It was massive, the size of the biggest Saint Bernard, covered in charcoal-colored fur—not black exactly, but like burned charcoal from a grill, that dark gray with hints of black. It held the coyote by the chest, and not a single part of the coyote's body touched the ground. This thing was so large it held a 40-pound animal like a terrier might hold a rat.

When Kyle's light hit it, the creature noticed him. It opened its mouth, dropping the dead coyote. And then it did something that shattered every natural law Kyle knew.

It stood up.

"It almost leans forward," Kyle told me, his voice still carrying the disbelief 18 years later, "like an old man standing up out of a rocking chair at Cracker Barrel somewhere on the porch. Real slow."

The thing towered over him—Kyle stands around 5′10″ and this creature stood at least 2 feet taller. Seven and a half, maybe 8 feet. Its chest and abdomen were shaped like a man's but covered in that charcoal fur. Blood ran down its chest "like hot candle wax dripping off a wick," fresh from the coyote it had been eating.

Kyle saw its hands pull up to its sides. Not paws. Hands. Like human hands but wrong, with long, claw-like fingers.

The face was wolf-like but attached to an upright body. The muzzle extended about 8 inches from its face. The ears sat more to the sides of its head than a normal wolf's, almost like a lynx or bobcat, but still distinctly canine. And the eyes—pitch black. Not reflecting Kyle's powerful light but absorbing it. "Darkness eternal, black holes," as Kyle described them.

The creature's mouth was wrong too. Where a dog's mouth ends at the back of the muzzle, this thing's mouth extended up onto the sides of its face. When it opened its jaws even partway, it looked like it was smiling—not from emotion, but from structure.

And then it took a step toward Kyle.

THE FIGHT FOR LIFE

Kyle ran. What else could a 15-year-old do when faced with a nightmare made flesh? He made it maybe 10 steps before Old Jake hit the creature broadside, throwing his full 120 pounds into it, snapping at it with those crushing jaws.

The dogman—because what else could you call it?—dealt with Jake with casual, terrible efficiency. One hand—Kyle specifically remembered it as a hand—pushed Jake away. Rolled him 4 or 5 feet like he was nothing, like swatting away a fly.

Then it continued pursuing Kyle.

Kyle was screaming for Jake to help him, running through the dark forest with only his light showing the path. Behind him, he could hear the creature gaining. It wasn't running exactly—it moved wrong, asymmetrical, but fast. Impossibly fast.

Jake hit it again, lunging with all his weight, trying to slow it down. Again, the creature threw him aside. Kyle could hear his dog's body hitting the ground, rolling through the leaves.

The third time Jake attacked, the creature grabbed him with both hands and threw him through the woods. Kyle heard his dog's body hitting low-hanging branches, crashing through underbrush. "Like a bag of trash," Kyle said. "It threw him through the woods like he was a bag of trash."

Kyle was certain Jake was dead. Nothing could survive that.

The creature was right on him now. Kyle could hear its breathing, feel its presence. He could smell it—not the smell of rot or death, but something specific and worse. The exact smell of vulture vomit, that unique stench that comes from birds that eat carrion. If you've ever walked up on a buzzard roost in the woods and smelled that particular combination of decay and digestive acids, you know there's nothing else like it.

Kyle tripped, falling face-first into a blown-down treetop. He rolled onto his back, trying to push himself backward through the brambles, and the creature dropped to all fours, bringing its face inches from his.

"I can see down the back of its throat," Kyle remembered. "I can see its teeth, its jawline, everything. This thing is snapping them jaws, that blood dripping, fresh blood, blowing blood and snot on me."

Kyle was still screaming for Jake, though he knew it was useless. His dog was dead. He was about to die. The gun on his back might as well have been a toy for all the good it would do against this thing.

And then, impossibly, Jake hit it again.

The old dog came in broadside, actually climbing on top of the creature. Kyle heard bones crunch—Jake had found something vital to bite. The creature let out a howl that Kyle felt in his chest, a sound that seemed to shake the earth itself, that rumbled through the ground and rattled the trees.

That's when Kyle ran for real. No looking back, no shining his light behind him. He made it maybe a hundred yards before he could hear the fight had changed again. The creature had Jake, and it was killing him. The sounds Kyle heard—he struggled to describe them even years later. The screams of a dog being torn apart, sounds that "pull your guts out."

Kyle pulled the .22 off his back and fired into the air, toward the cliffs, away from Jake but loud enough to be heard. "Come on, Jake!" he screamed. "Come on, let's go home!"

Then silence. Complete silence. No crickets, no frogs, no night birds. The forest itself seemed to hold its breath.

THE IMPOSSIBLE RETURN

Kyle made it to the truck in shock, covered in dirt and sweat, tears running down his face. His grandfather took one look at him and knew something terrible had happened. As Kyle tried to explain—a monster, a werewolf, something impossible—his grandfather started the truck.

"If what you told me is true," the old man said, "then we have to come back and get Jake. We have to."

Kyle tried to argue. Jake was dead. He'd heard him being killed. But his grandfather possessed wisdom that came from a lifetime in these mountains. He threw his jacket out the truck window—Jake knew his scent and would lie on it if he somehow survived.

"He fought for your life four times," Papaw said. "Four times he fought for your life. He did it out of love for you. We have to come back and look for him."

Then he said something that Kyle would carry forever: "Listen, there's things in these woods that I cannot explain. I've hunted these woods my whole entire life. But if you want to hunt, if you want to fish and dig ginseng, look for mushrooms and do man stuff, you've got to come to terms with it. If you want to do what you love, you have to come to terms with it."

They returned at dawn, Kyle never leaving the truck, calling for the dogs. Nothing. They came back that evening. Still nothing. Finally, as darkness was falling on the second day, Kyle's grandfather saw movement in the woods.

"There's Bo," he said, seeing the red tickhound moving slowly through the trees.

Kyle grabbed a leash and started walking toward the dog. But as he got closer, he realized it wasn't Bo at all.

It was Jake.

The dog was unrecognizable. He was covered head to toe in blood. His nose was nearly torn off, hanging sideways on his face. His chest was ripped open to the chest plate. Both ears looked like "freshly cooked ramen noodles," just strips of meat hanging down. His right hip was fractured. He walked with a severe limp. Big gash marks ran down his back and hips. Most of his tail was gone. His collar was missing.

By every measure of logic and biology, Jake should have been dead. But somehow, impossibly, he was walking. Kyle's grandfather—this tough mountain man who'd never shown much emotion—bent down and picked up all 120 pounds of

Jake's broken body and carried him to the truck. Not to the dog box, but laid him gently in the truck bed.

For three weeks, Kyle's grandmother kept Jake in the house, doctoring him with everything she knew. Gatorade for hydration, superglue for the ears, constant cleaning, and bandaging. The extended family came to see him, amazed that he was alive.

And not only did Jake survive—he recovered enough to hunt again. He lived for years afterward, though never quite the same. His legendary status in the community was replaced by something else: awe that he had survived at all.

THE DEPTH OF THE BOND

"The only thing I can think that pulled him through," Kyle told me, "was the love that he had for us."

This part of Kyle's story hit me differently from the encounter itself. For years after that night, Kyle struggled not just with what he'd seen but with guilt. If his grandfather hadn't possessed the wisdom to go back, Kyle would have left Jake to die alone in those woods. The dog that had saved his life four times would have died abandoned.

Kyle self-medicated with alcohol for years, not because of the trauma of the encounter, but because of what Jake's sacrifice meant. A love so pure it would face death repeatedly without hesitation. A loyalty that transcended species, that spoke to something deeper than evolution could explain.

"There's not a person listening to this right now," Kyle said during our interview, "that if they were in my shoes would have known what to do that early in life."

He was right. How do you process that kind of love, that kind of sacrifice, when you're 15 years old and you've just discovered that monsters are real?

Bo was found two weeks later at a local market, thin but relatively unhurt. He'd run that night and survived. No one blamed him—he was young, untested. But Jake had stood his ground against the impossible.

THE INVITATION

As Kyle finished his story during our interview, I found myself doing something I rarely did back then.

"If I came to Kentucky," I asked, "would you show me where this happened?"

I expected him to decline. Who would want to return to a place where they'd nearly been killed by something that shouldn't exist? The trauma was still visible in Kyle's voice 18 years later. But his answer surprised me.

"Yes," he said. "But you're gonna need to bring an army."

That's how I found myself, in October 2021, driving through the Pennsylvania mountains at two in the morning, heading to Kentucky with enough ammunition to supply a small militia, listening to a podcast that would completely reframe everything I thought I knew about dogmen.

THE PORTAL REVELATION

Tim Pool had a guest on his show—Shane Cashman, a journalist who was starting a paranormal podcast. During their conversation, Shane mentioned interviewing a witch who'd attended a school of mystery. These are real places where people learn actual witchcraft, not the Hollywood version, but the ancient practices that open doors between worlds.

This witch told Shane that during a class on opening portals, they'd succeeded. And through that portal walked an upright dog.

I was alone in my truck, surrounded by Pennsylvania forest in the dead of night, heading to hunt for the same type of creature this witch claimed came from another realm. I looked in my rearview mirror at the cases of ammunition I'd brought, thinking about the physical creature Kyle had described, and realized I might be preparing for the wrong kind of battle entirely.

What if dogmen weren't just undiscovered animals living in our forests? What if they were something that moved between worlds?

INTO THE DANIEL BOONE

October 2021. I arrived in Kentucky with my team—Ward, our cameraman; Joel and Christian, both armed and ready for whatever we might encounter. We met Kyle at his property, and immediately, I could see the weight this experience still carried for him. Eighteen years had passed, but when he talked about that night, he was 15 again, alone in the darkness with a nightmare.

Kyle agreed to take us to the location during daylight but made it clear he wouldn't stay after dark. "You can camp out there if you want," he said, "but I won't be there."

The logging road his grandfather had driven down that night was supposed to be open, but when we arrived, the gate was locked. We had to hike in—miles through the forest, carrying our gear, racing against the dying light. By the time we reached the spot where Kyle's grandfather had parked that night, it was already too late to go deeper. We had to hike Kyle out before darkness fell, then return without him.

WHEN THE FOREST RESPONDED

As we hiked deeper into the Daniel Boone, something strange happened. Joel and Christian had walked ahead around a curve in the logging road while Kyle and I started up a hill to check out a watering hole. That's when I heard shouting from below.

Joel was visibly shaken when I reached him. He and Christian had witnessed a massive tree—three feet in diameter—violently shaking with no visible cause. Nothing else moved. No wind. No other trees. Just this one giant oak, swaying and shaking as if grabbed by invisible hands.

"It was like something huge was shaking it," Joel said, still trying to process what he'd seen. "But there was nothing there."

Christian had tried to film it, but by the time he got his camera up, the shaking had stopped. The forest had gone completely still, that heavy silence that makes you feel like you're being watched.

This was my first indication that the Daniel Boone National Forest might be what Michael Heiser calls a "sacred space"—a place where the boundaries between the spiritual and physical realms are particularly thin. Not sacred in a holy sense, but in the ancient understanding of places where Heaven and earth overlap, where the normal rules don't quite apply.

THE LAST NIGHT

On our final night in Kentucky, we decided to try something desperate. If this thing was out there, we'd try to lure it in. We bought steaks from a supermarket and fishing line. Christian and I took position on a ridge with night vision while Joel and Ward went down to hang the meat from trees near where the tree had shaken.

When they returned, both men were rattled. As they'd been hanging the bait, something had rushed through the canopy above them—not wind, but a directed force that moved from tree to tree directly overhead.

"It was like something huge moving through the tops of the trees," Ward said, "but we couldn't see anything."

We stayed on that ridge until nearly dawn, watching, waiting. Nothing showed itself. But the forest felt alive in a way that defied explanation, as if we were being observed by intelligences that chose not to reveal themselves.

THE FOOTSTEPS IN MY HOME

Months later, we were preparing to release our documentary about the Kentucky expedition. Lindsay and I were in our basement discussing final details when we went upstairs to the kitchen. Our house had hardwood floors throughout the first level, carpet upstairs. Our only pet was a declawed cat who was sitting right beside me.

That's when we heard it—heavy, bipedal footsteps crossing our hardwood floor. But these weren't human footsteps. With each step came the distinct sound of claws clicking against the wood. The footfalls were so heavy that both Lindsay and I felt the vibrations through the floor.

"Did you hear that?" I asked, though her wide eyes already gave me the answer.

"I didn't just hear it," she said. "I felt it."

Something had walked through our home. Something with weight, with claws, with intention. Something that wasn't entirely in our physical realm but could still affect it. The investigation into Kyle's encounter hadn't just documented a historical event—it had drawn attention.

THE PATTERN EMERGES

Through Kyle's encounter, our investigation, and the experiences that followed, a pattern became clear. Dogmen aren't simply undiscovered animals living in our forests. They're something far more complex and disturbing.

Kyle's dogman exhibited intelligence, walking upright when it chose to, understanding that Kyle was a witness to eliminate. The tree shaking in broad daylight suggested something that could affect our physical world while remaining unseen. The rushing force through the canopy, the footsteps in my home—all of it pointed to entities that operate between dimensions.

This aligns with what I'd discovered through other investigations. Some witnesses describe dogmen that appear and disappear without using any visible entrance or exit. Others report them in places where they couldn't possibly remain hidden—urban areas, small patches of woods surrounded by development. The only explanation that fits all the data is that these beings can move between our physical realm and somewhere else.

The Daniel Boone National Forest, like many wilderness areas where dogmen are repeatedly encountered, seems to be more than just habitat. These may be boundary zones, places where our reality touches something else. In Heiser's framework, certain geographical locations have always been understood as points of intersection between the human and divine realms—mountains, wilderness areas, isolated forests.

THE PROTECTION IN THE PATTERN

Throughout Kyle's encounter, despite the dogman's overwhelming physical superiority, boundaries were maintained. The creature could pursue but not catch. It could injure Jake but not kill him. It could terrorize but not destroy.

This pattern appears consistently across legitimate dogman encounters. These entities seem to operate under restrictions, able to manifest and frighten but rarely able to kill. It's as if they're on a leash, permitted to go so far but no further.

Old Jake's survival defied every natural law. A 120-pound dog thrown multiple times by a creature of immense strength, his body broken and torn, somehow walked out of those woods alive. Kyle's grandmother said it was love that pulled him through, and she wasn't wrong. But there was something more—a boundary that couldn't be crossed, a line the enemy couldn't pass.

THE ONGOING REALITY

Episode 335, "Dog vs. Dogman," became one of the most talked-about episodes in *The Confessionals'* history. Not because it was the most dramatic—we've had wilder stories—but because it revealed something fundamental about the nature of these entities and the spiritual war we're all part of.

These things are real. They can affect our physical world. They can leave claw marks and footprints, kill coyotes, and chase teenagers through the forest. But they're not just physical. They move between realms, operate under spiritual authority, and seem particularly interested in those who investigate them.

The footsteps in my home weren't a coincidence. They were a message: We know who you are. We know what you're doing. We can reach you.

But those footsteps also revealed a limitation. They could walk through my home, but they couldn't harm my family. They could make their presence known, but they couldn't cross the boundary of divine protection. Greater is He (God) who is in us than he that is in the world (1 John 4:4).

Every person who accepts that these entities exist, who understands that the spiritual realm actively interfaces with our physical world, is faced with a choice. If the darkness is real, if these fallen beings can manifest in our reality, then the light must be real too. If there are demons, there must be God. If there is a cosmic rebellion, there must be a divine authority they're rebelling against.

Kyle's encounter wasn't just a random attack by an undiscovered cryptid. It was an intersection between our world and the spiritual realm, a moment when the veil thinned enough for a 15-year-old boy to see what moves in the darkness. But it was also a testimony to protection, to boundaries that evil cannot cross, to a love that throws itself between us and the monsters.

The war is real. The enemy is real. But so is the protection available to those who call on the name of Jesus Christ.

That's the ultimate truth behind every dogman encounter, every cryptid sighting, every paranormal experience. We're not alone in this universe. There are forces of incredible darkness that hate humanity and seek our destruction. But there's also the God who loves us, who sent His Son to die for us, who offers protection and salvation to all who believe.

The choice, as always, is ours.

THE MISSING PIECE

Kyle's encounter in the Daniel Boone National Forest had opened a door in my understanding, but it was still incomplete. His encounter provides the physical side of the story—a dogman had hunted a 15-year-old boy through those Kentucky woods. But the patterns I'd been tracking across hundreds of episodes suggested something more complex. The tree shaking with no visible cause. The rushing force through the canopy during our investigation. The footsteps in my home after we'd returned. All of it pointed toward entities that could operate between dimensions, not just within our physical realm. The theory was forming, but I needed confirmation—a case that would prove definitively that these creatures weren't just flesh and blood, no matter how impossible their flesh and blood might be.

That confirmation arrived in my inbox in early 2022.

The email came from a worship pastor in middle Tennessee named Hunter. Unlike most witnesses who struggle to articulate their experiences, Hunter laid out his encounter with methodical precision. He'd seen a dogman—that much was familiar. But the circumstances of his sighting shattered the boundaries between dream and reality in ways I'd never encountered before.

"I thought it was just a dream," he wrote, "until I woke up with claw marks on my back."

Physical wounds from a dream encounter. If Hunter's account was true—and the details he provided suggested it was—then we had proof. Not speculation, not theory, but evidence that dogmen could attack in one realm and leave their marks in another. They weren't just interdimensional travelers; they could engage with humans across dimensional boundaries, hunting in dreams and leaving scars in the waking world.

This was the piece I'd been searching for, the confirmation of this journey I had gone on with Kyle, which I had suspected. Dogmen weren't confined to our reality. They moved through it.

Hunter's story would transform everything I thought I knew about the nature of these entities and the war we're all part of, whether we see it or not.

8

When Dreams Leave Scars

For we wrestle not against flesh and blood, but against principalities, against powers, against the rulers of the darkness of this world, against spiritual wickedness in high places.

—Ephesians 6:12 KJV

The scratches on Hunter's back told a different story than his mind wanted to believe.

Standing in his bathroom that Saturday morning in early 2022, the Tennessee pastor and contractor stared at his reflection, trying to reconcile what his wife was seeing with what he remembered from the night before. Three distinct claw marks raked across his back, still raw and angry. His right shoulder bore the purple-blue bruising of what looked unmistakably like finger marks—three or four of them, pressed deep enough into his flesh to leave their testimony.

"I thought it was just a dream," Hunter would later tell me, his voice carrying the weight of a man whose reality had fundamentally shifted. But dreams don't leave physical evidence. Dreams don't mark you.

Or do they?

The question would haunt Hunter for months, reshaping his understanding of reality itself. As a deacon in his church, a successful contractor running his own business, a father coaching his children's sports teams, Hunter had built his life on solid, tangible foundations. You measure twice, cut once. You pour concrete on level ground. You trust what you can see, touch, and verify. But those scratches on his back challenged everything he thought he knew about the boundaries between the physical and spiritual worlds.

THE VISION THAT BLED THROUGH

Hunter's experience began in what he called the dream state, though even his description of it challenged conventional understanding. "It's more real than real life," he explained during our first conversation. "I can smell things, I can feel things. I feel the wind blowing. It's just as real, if not more real than me sitting here right now."

This hyperreality of the experience sets it apart from ordinary dreams. Neuroscience tells us that normal dreams, while sometimes vivid, lack certain sensory details—we rarely smell in dreams, rarely feel texture or temperature with clarity. But Hunter's experience contained all these elements and more, suggesting he had accessed something beyond the typical dream state.

In this vision, Hunter found himself in his front yard on what seemed like an ordinary day. His wife sat on the front steps of their home while their children played nearby. Hunter had walked over to the creek that runs through their property with his son, examining something in the water—a moment of simple father-son connection that could have happened any weekend.

But when Hunter looked up from the creek, his son had already walked back to join his mother and sibling. That's when Hunter noticed it: across the street, behind a large hedge, stood something that violated every law of nature he knew. The figure was massive, black, wolf-like, but fundamentally wrong—standing upright like a man, its form partially concealed but unmistakably predatory.

"I remember thinking, *I'm seeing things,*" Hunter recalled. The creature wasn't looking at him. Its attention was locked entirely on his family with an intensity that triggered every protective instinct in Hunter's body. He yelled for his wife and children to get in the house, but they couldn't see what he saw. To them, their husband and father was shouting about nothing, gesturing at empty air.

THE SPEED OF DARKNESS

What happened next revealed the true nature of the threat. The creature moved with impossible speed—not running but somehow flowing, "like a freaking blur," as Hunter described it. In the space of two or three seconds, it had circled around, positioning itself between Hunter and his family.

Hunter didn't hesitate. In that moment, whether in body or spirit, Hunter embodied the Scripture: *"Greater love hath no man than this, that a man lay down his life for his friends"* (John 15:13 KJV). He charged at the creature, attempting to intercept it before it could reach his wife and children.

The physical contact was visceral and specific. The entity grabbed Hunter's right shoulder with what he distinctly remembered as a hand—not a paw, not a claw, but a hand with long, bony fingers that possessed tremendous strength. It threw him to the ground with casual violence, the impact driving the air from his lungs even in this strange realm between dreams and reality.

Then came the claws. As Hunter struggled on the ground, he felt them rake across his back—three deliberate strokes that burned like fire. The pain was immediate and intense, not the muted sensation of a dream but the sharp, specific agony of flesh being torn.

Then he woke up, sitting bolt upright in bed, his heart hammering, sheets soaked with sweat.

THE MORNING REVELATION

Hunter might have dismissed the entire experience as an extraordinarily vivid nightmare—his mind processing some unknown stress or fear—except for what his wife discovered that morning. As Hunter stood in their bathroom preparing to shower, she walked in and stopped mid-sentence.

"What happened to your back? You're bleeding."

The scratches were real. Three parallel marks, exactly where the creature had clawed him in the "dream." The bruising on his shoulder matched precisely where those inhuman fingers had gripped him. Hunter had gone to sleep unmarked and awakened wounded by something that shouldn't exist.

This intersection of dream and physical reality appears throughout Scripture, though we often gloss over its implications. Jacob wrestled with an angel through the night and walked with a limp for the rest of his life—his spiritual encounter left permanent physical consequences. Daniel became physically ill for days after his visions. The apostle Paul wrote of being *"caught up to the third heaven,"* unable to determine if the experience was physical or spiritual: *"...(whether in the body, I cannot tell; or whether out of the body, I cannot tell: God knoweth)"* (2 Corinthians 12:2 KJV).

The spiritual realm has always had the power to affect the physical, but we've trained ourselves to ignore or explain away these intersections.

THE PHYSICAL GATEWAY

Hunter's case presents a fascinating physiological component that may explain his susceptibility to these experiences. His heart rate regularly drops into the 30s while sleeping, sometimes dipping as low as 32 beats per minute—a condition that places his body in a state remarkably similar to the threshold between life and death.

"Your brain will kind of begin to shut down," Hunter explained, "and it releases a certain chemical which is the same chemical that is released when you're in REM sleep or when you die."

This detail cannot be overlooked. Modern science has identified dimethyltryptamine (DMT) as the chemical released during death, dreams, and near-death experiences. Some researchers call it "the spirit molecule" because of its apparent ability to facilitate experiences beyond ordinary consciousness. Hunter's naturally low heart rate may trigger this release more frequently or intensely than normal, creating an involuntary gateway between realms.

Hunter's near-death heart rate may serve as an involuntary opening, thinning the veil between our realm and what

Scripture identifies as the second heaven—that contested spiritual territory where dark forces operate. Unlike those who deliberately pursue astral projection through forbidden occult practices, Hunter found himself pulled into these experiences without invitation or intent.

His Apple Watch, which he wears constantly to monitor his condition, has logged over 250 low heart rate warnings. The pattern became clear over time: when his heart rate drops below 35 beats per minute and remains there, these experiences intensify. The correlation is too consistent to ignore.

TWO MONTHS LATER: THE WOODS CONFIRM THE WARNING

April 10, 2022. The early spring air carried the promise of new growth as Hunter and his 11-year-old son ventured into the woods behind their home. These 800 acres of Tennessee wilderness weren't just property—they were legacy. Hunter's sister had married into the family that owned this land when he was just 10 years old. For 25 years, these woods had been his sanctuary, the place where his father taught him to track deer, where he'd learned patience in tree stands, where generations of his family had walked before him.

That afternoon started like countless others. Father and son checking trail cameras, looking for signs of deer, enjoying the simple pleasure of being outdoors together. Hunter had been passing down the same traditions his father had given him—teaching his boy to read signs, to move quietly through the forest, to respect the land and its creatures.

The light was already beginning to fade when they reached the hollow where their tree stand waited. It was maybe 4:00 or

4:30, Hunter recalled, that golden hour when the afternoon sun slants through the trees at sharp angles, creating long shadows that can play tricks on your eyes.

The whispers began subtly, so faint at first that Hunter thought it might be wind through the early spring leaves. But wind doesn't form words. Wind doesn't sound like conversation just beyond the range of understanding.

"It sounded like gibberish or like another language," Hunter recalled, his voice still carrying wonder and fear at the memory. The unintelligible vocalizations seemed to shift positions—behind them, then ahead, then surrounding them entirely. Father and son stood frozen, trying to locate the source, but the whispers seemed to come from everywhere and nowhere simultaneously.

THE LANGUAGE OF THE FALLEN

This phenomenon appears throughout cryptid encounters worldwide, crossing cultural and geographical boundaries with disturbing consistency. The Sierra Sounds, recorded by Ron Moorehead in the 1970s in California's Sierra Nevada mountains, captured similar unintelligible speech attributed to Sasquatch. Witnesses across hundreds of cases describe this same element: a language that sounds structured, deliberate, even conversational, but remains completely incomprehensible to human ears.

Could these be the remnants of pre-Babel communication, when the whole earth spoke one language? Or perhaps something older still—the tongue of the Nephilim, those hybrid beings from before the flood whose very existence violated the boundary between Heaven and earth? The book of Enoch, while not canonical, suggests these beings possessed knowledge and abilities that blended the spiritual and physical in ways that threatened the created order itself.

As darkness settled through the trees, the whispers ceased. The sudden silence was almost worse than the voices—that heavy, expectant quiet that falls over a forest when a predator is near. Every seasoned hunter knows this silence. Birds stop singing. Squirrels freeze on their branches. Even the insects seem to hold their breath.

Then came the sound of breaking branches, not the random noise of wind or small animals, but the deliberate sound of something large moving through the underbrush. Hunter motioned for his son to be still. On the count of three, they would shine their flashlights toward the disturbance.

"One...two...three."

Their flashlight beams pierced the darkness, and two orange-red orbs rose from behind the undergrowth—eyes that didn't just reflect their lights but seemed to glow with their own inner fire. As the creature stood to its full height, Hunter's mind struggled to process what he was seeing.

"The only thing I can tell you is a werewolf," Hunter said during our interview, his voice dropping to barely above a whisper. "This thing...it was just a black wolf standing up on two legs."

THE RECOGNITION

In that moment of terror, something else happened—recognition. This was the same creature from his dream two months earlier. The same impossible blend of wolf and man, the same predatory focus, the same overwhelming sense of evil. But this time it wasn't targeting his family. This time, it was looking directly at him and his son.

The creature released a sound Hunter struggled to describe even months later. He first compared it to what he imagined a dinosaur might sound like—something primitive and terrible. Later, he refined the description to the deep, guttural roar of a crocodile, that prehistoric bellow that speaks to something ancient in the human nervous system, triggering fear responses laid down in our DNA millions of years ago.

The apostle Peter's warning took on visceral meaning in that moment: *"Be sober, be vigilant; because your adversary the devil, as a roaring lion, walketh about, seeking whom he may devour"* (1 Peter 5:8 KJV). This wasn't metaphorical spiritual warfare—this was a physical manifestation of something that should have remained in the spiritual realm.

Hunter's son reacted faster than his father. While Hunter stood transfixed, his mind reeling from the impossibility of what he was seeing, the 11-year-old boy was already tugging at his father's arm. "Dad, dad, dad, we need to go."

The boy's urgency snapped Hunter back to the present danger. They began backing away slowly, fighting every instinct that screamed at them to run. Every hunter knows you don't run from a predator. Running triggers the chase instinct. Running makes you prey.

DIVINE PROTECTION IN DARK WOODS

The creature didn't charge immediately. Instead, it paced them as they retreated, maintaining its distance but ensuring its presence was felt with each deliberate step. It would take a few steps parallel to their path, then stop. They would back up further. It would move again, always keeping them in sight, always maintaining that careful distance that suggested calculation rather than mere animal instinct.

This restraint appears repeatedly in dogman encounters across the country, suggesting these entities operate under divine limitations. The book of Job provides biblical precedent: when satan sought to test Job, God set clear boundaries: *"Behold, all that he hath is in thy power; only upon himself put not forth thine hand"* (Job 1:12 KJV). Even the fallen must operate within boundaries set by the Almighty. They can manifest, they can terrorize, but something—Someone—prevents them from taking what they seem to want.

Hunter and his son continued their careful retreat until they reached the edge of the woods where it opened into a 50-acre hay field. The moment they broke from the tree line into the open space, they ran. That's when Hunter heard it—the sound of something large crashing through the underbrush behind them, no longer pacing but pursuing.

Without breaking stride, Hunter drew his pistol and fired several shots behind them into the darkness. He doesn't know if he hit anything. In that moment, accuracy didn't matter—only escape. Father and son ran across that field faster than they'd ever run before, not stopping until they reached the safety of their house.

THE AFTERMATH OF IMPOSSIBILITY

Inside, as Hunter and his son caught their breath, his wife's words brought everything full circle: "Didn't you have a dream about exactly what you're talking about?"

The connection hit Hunter like a physical blow. The creature in his dream, the one that had left physical scratches on his back, wasn't a projection of his subconscious or a symbolic representation of some psychological fear. It was a real entity that could operate in both the dream realm and physical reality. The warning had been literal. The threat was real.

THE MULTI-ORIGIN MYSTERY

The complexity of the dogman phenomenon reflects the multifaceted nature of spiritual warfare itself. Through six years of documenting these encounters on *The Confessionals,* I've identified several potential origins for these creatures, each supported by eyewitness testimony and patterns of behavior.

Nephilim Spirits: Genesis 6 speaks of the Nephilim, the hybrid offspring of fallen angels and human women. The phrase "and also after that" suggests these beings continued to exist even after the initial hybridization event. The book of Enoch, though not canonical, provides additional detail, suggesting these beings' spirits were condemned to remain on Earth after death. Could some dogmen be these disembodied Nephilim taking physical form?

Government Assets: Multiple witnesses have reported encounters with government agents after dogman sightings or shootings. One particularly compelling case involved a trucker who shot and killed a dogman that was pacing his vehicle. Shortly after, unmarked vehicles arrived, and agents told him he had "killed their asset." This suggests at least some dogmen might be products of classified military experiments—biological weapons or genetically modified organisms created through dark knowledge, whether ancient or modern.

Human Shapeshifters: I've documented cases of humans who transform through occult practices. One source described dating a woman who was part of a group of shapeshifters, and detailed territorial wars between different factions across state lines, including specific conflicts between Tennessee and Kentucky groups. This transformation ability brings to mind the boundary between human and beast being violated through spiritual means.

Interdimensional Avatars: Perhaps most disturbing is the possibility that some dogmen are biological vessels—*meat suits*, as one witness described them—created in other realms and inhabited by fallen entities when they need to operate physically in our world. These would be purpose-built bodies designed for specific missions in our reality.

The variety of origins suggests we're not dealing with a single phenomenon but rather multiple types of entities that share similar physical characteristics. They may serve different masters, operate under different rules, and pursue different agendas, though all seem aligned against humanity in some fashion.

THE BLOOD TESTAMENT

Hunter carries Rh-negative blood, a type shared by only 15 percent of the global population. This blood type appears with unusual frequency among those who report paranormal and interdimensional experiences. Some researchers suggest, those with Rh-negative blood report at rates approaching 90 percent, far beyond what chance would suggest.

Some researchers connect this to the Nephilim bloodlines, suggesting Rh-negative blood carries genetic markers from before the flood. In the Basque region of Spain and France,

Rh-negative blood appears as high as approximately 35 percent, far above the global average, and the people speak Euskera—a language that predates all other European languages and has no known linguistic relatives. Could this be a remnant of pre-Babel speech, preserved in a population that carries ancient genetic markers?

If blood carries life, as Scripture states, might it also carry spiritual markers, generational blessings or curses passed through family lines? Hunter's mother shared his ability to perceive spiritual realities in their haunted childhood home. His father, lacking this bloodline, remained blind to the supernatural activity happening around him.

This hereditary sensitivity suggests that some families carry a particular susceptibility to interdimensional contact, possibly written into their very DNA. Hunter's low body temperature, another marker associated with Rh-negative blood, compounds this susceptibility. The implications are staggering: are some people born with a thinner veil between themselves and the spiritual realm?

THE WITNESS OF TWO

Hunter's 11-year-old son saw the same entity, heard the same otherworldly sounds, felt the same overwhelming evil. This shared testimony eliminates hallucination or mental illness as explanations. Whatever stood in those Tennessee woods that April evening was real enough to be perceived by two separate consciousnesses, substantial enough to trigger the primal fear response in both father and son.

For the boy, this encounter became an unwanted initiation into spiritual reality. At 11 years old, he discovered that the world contains active evil that can take physical form. How does a child process such knowledge? How does he return to school, to playing with friends, knowing that monsters are real and can step out of nightmares into the waking world?

Hunter chose not to press his son for details, not wanting to traumatize him further. But occasionally, carefully, he would check in. The boy remembered everything but preferred not to discuss it, a common response among young witnesses to supernatural events. The experience had marked him, changed him, and initiated him into a reality that most people can comfortably deny.

THE PATTERN AND THE PROMISE

Hunter's progression follows a pattern I've documented across hundreds of cases on *The Confessionals:*

1. *Initial Contact:* Often through dreams or peripheral experiences.
2. *Physical Confirmation:* Unexplained marks, injuries, or evidence that something crossed from the spiritual to physical.
3. *Escalation:* Direct sighting or confrontation in our physical realm.
4. *Revelation:* Understanding that reality is far more complex and dangerous than previously believed.
5. *Spiritual Reckoning:* Recognizing the need for divine protection and the reality of spiritual warfare.

The scratches on Hunter's back weren't just wounds—they were signatures, proof that the barrier between realms is far more permeable than we imagine. They were warnings that the spiritual war described in Scripture isn't metaphorical but literal, not distant but intimate, not ancient history but present reality.

Yet Scripture offers hope throughout this darkness: *"He that dwelleth in the secret place of the most High shall abide under the shadow of the Almighty"* (Psalm 91:1 KJV). Hunter would learn to lean on these promises in the months that followed, as the experiences continued and intensified. The name of Jesus became his shield, the only defense that seemed to matter when facing entities that could move between realms at will.

When Hunter returned to share what God had shown him about the spiritual warfare headed my way—a prophecy delivered through a dream about my own home—it would transform my understanding of the battle we're all in, whether we recognize it or not. The hooded figures he saw following me into my house would later be identified by Pastor Dave Bryan as druids, witches operating in the physical realm but serving spiritual masters. The war wasn't just interdimensional; it involved human agents as well.

The scratches healed, leaving only faint marks on Hunter's back. But the knowledge they represented would never fade. The veil had been torn, and Hunter had seen what moves behind it. There was no going back to ignorance, no return to the comfortable illusion that the material world is all that exists.

The dreams that leave scars teach us that the battlefield extends beyond what we can see, into realms we visit every night when we close our eyes. And sometimes, what we encounter there follows us home.

THE VISION WITHHELD

But Hunter's experiences weren't finished. In the months that followed, as the interdimensional intrusions intensified to weekly occurrences, something else began to emerge—visions that weren't about him at all. Dreams that felt different from his usual encounters, carrying a weight of purpose rather than threat.

In July 2023, a year after his physical encounter with the dogman in the woods, Hunter experienced what he would later describe as the most vivid and specific vision of his life. He saw a house he'd never visited, witnessed spiritual enemies following someone he'd never met, and received a warning that wasn't for him but through him.

The vision troubled him for weeks. He'd seen me—Tony Merkel, host of *The Confessionals*—though we'd never met in person. He'd seen my house in perfect detail, down to the gray vinyl siding and the curved road. Most disturbing, he'd seen two hooded figures following me into my home.

Hunter wrestled with what to do. How do you tell someone you've never met that you've had a prophetic dream about them? How do you explain that God has shown you their house, their vulnerability, their spiritual enemies?

For more than a year, Hunter carried this burden. He prayed about it, discussed it with his wife, and tried to dismiss it as his imagination. But the vision's clarity never faded. If anything, it grew more urgent with time. The sense that he needed to deliver this warning intensified until he couldn't ignore it anymore.

Over a year after the vision, Hunter finally reached out to me again, knowing he had to come to the studio to speak with me about this. Some messages can't wait for convenience. Some warnings must be delivered face-to-face.

9

When the Veil Speaks

For the Lord God does nothing without revealing his secret to his servants the prophets.

—Amos 3:7 ESV

Hunter's hands trembled slightly as he sat across from me in the studio, 18 months after our first conversation. The contractor-turned-worship pastor had driven four hours from middle Tennessee despite working 60 hours that week, compelled by something he couldn't quite name. Now, surrounded by my team—Ward, Joel, and Jack—he was about to share something that would fundamentally alter my understanding of the spiritual battle I'd been sensing for over a year.

"I don't know how to ask this without..." Hunter paused, searching for words. The normally confident man who ran his own construction company and led worship at his church seemed suddenly uncertain.

"Just ask it, dude," I told him.

Hunter took a breath. "The number [REDACTED]. Does that mean anything to you?"

The studio went silent. My heart stopped. That was my house number.

"We can't talk about this on the show," I said, my voice catching. "But the answer is yes."

The weight of the moment crashed over me. This wasn't someone claiming to have a word from God that could apply to anyone. This was specific, verifiable, and impossible to fake. I felt tears welling up—not from fear, but from the overwhelming confirmation of what I'd been sensing for months.

THE DREAM THAT CROSSED BOUNDARIES

July 6, 2023. While Hunter slept on his couch in middle Tennessee, something pulled his consciousness 200 miles east to a house he'd never seen, to witness something that hadn't yet happened—or perhaps was happening in a realm just beyond our perception.

"I was at church first," Hunter explained, his voice steadier now that he knew I was taking him seriously. "I'd just taken over as youth worship leader, and I was dreaming about being there. Then it's almost like it jumped—like I went straight from the church to this other place."

The transition itself was significant. From a place of worship to a scene of spiritual warfare. From holy ground to contested territory. The sequence wouldn't make sense until later, when Pastor Dave Bryan would explain what Hunter had actually witnessed.

"I'm at the end of this curved road," Hunter continued, "and at the corner, there's a driveway with a house that sits way back from the street."

My house. Exactly my house. Set back from the road in a way that made it unique on our street, positioned at the curve he described perfectly.

"I see you getting out of a dark truck," Hunter said. "And there's these two cloaked figures. Dark. I couldn't see faces, just side profiles. And they're following you."

Ward leaned forward. "Following him where?"

"Around the back of the house. Not through the front door—around the back."

The detail was unnervingly specific. Our front door faces the street, but we almost never use it. Family and friends know to come around back, through the gate, to the door we actually use. How could Hunter know this?

"What color was the house?" I pressed, needing more confirmation.

"Gray and white. I remember it being gray. Not brick, not vinyl—well, it looked like wood, but it was gray. And there was white trim, with a peak above the steps."

Every detail matched. Even his confusion about the material—our vinyl siding has a wood grain texture that makes it look like painted wood from a distance.

THE BIBLICAL PATTERN OF WARNING DREAMS

Throughout Scripture, God has used dreams to warn His servants of impending danger. Joseph's dreams saved not only his family but entire nations from famine. Daniel's visions revealed the rise and fall of kingdoms. But perhaps most relevant to Hunter's experience was the pattern of dreams warning about immediate, personal danger.

Consider Joseph, the earthly father of Jesus, who received multiple warning dreams. "*...the angel of the Lord appeareth to Joseph in a dream, saying, Arise, and take the young child and his mother, and flee into Egypt, and be thou there until I bring thee word: for Herod will seek the young child to destroy him*" (Matthew 2:13 KJV). The dream was specific, actionable, and warned of human agents working against God's purposes.

This pattern—divine warning through dreams about human opposition—appears throughout biblical history. God warned Abimelech in a dream about Abraham's wife. He warned the wise men not to return to Herod. He warned Pilate's wife about Jesus. In each case, the dream served as divine intervention, revealing hidden dangers that natural perception couldn't detect.

Hunter's dream fit this biblical pattern precisely. It revealed human agents (the druids) operating in the spiritual realm, following me into my home with malicious intent. Like Joseph's dream about Herod, it warned of organized human opposition working through spiritual means.

THE CONFIRMATION SKETCH

Three days after Hunter's visit to the studio, I received a text that stopped me cold. He'd drawn what he saw in the dream—a sketch of my house that was 98 percent accurate. Details that shouldn't be possible for him to know were there on the paper: the vertical vinyl siding that looks like wood, the gray and white color scheme, the peaked entrance over the front steps, and even the way the houses on either side sit at different elevations.

But it wasn't just one sketch. Hunter had drawn three different perspectives: the front of my house, a side view, and even a portion of my neighbor's house. The neighbor's house sketch showed a steep incline of a hill with specific architectural details that Hunter labeled "house to the left." When I realized he'd drawn my neighbor's house, the accuracy was stunning—down to the fence line and the way their property slopes.

Most telling was what he got wrong: he placed my house number by the front door when it actually sits on my mailbox at the street. The kind of minor transposition that often happens in genuine remote viewing, where the mind correctly identifies elements but sometimes misplaces them spatially.

I had to ask him directly: "If you're lying to me, if you're just clowning around, just tell me. I'm not going to be mad. I just want to know."

His response carried a hint of hurt. "Tony, do you know how busy my life is? Do you think I have time to drive four hours to stake out your house for some elaborate prank?"

He was right. The logistics alone made deception nearly impossible. Google Street View couldn't help him—our houses were built after the last time Google's cameras came through. Our neighborhood doesn't exist on the internet in any searchable form. To know these details, he would have had to physically visit, study the property, take notes or photos, then wait over a year for the perfect moment to reveal his "prophecy." The idea was absurd.

THE GRAY OBSERVER ENCOUNTER

Hunter's experiences had escalated dramatically since our first interview. The windmill sound—that distinctive whomp-whomp-whomp that preceded his interdimensional experiences—now occurred weekly. But a recent event had crossed a disturbing new threshold.

"I fell asleep on the couch," Hunter recounted, his voice dropping as he relived the experience.

"My wife went to bed, didn't want to wake me. I'm dead asleep when something wakes me up. First thing I notice is that sound—like a giant fan or helicopter blade moving really slow."

The sound was his warning now, the herald of an interdimensional intrusion. But this time was different.

"I wake up and I'm looking at the ceiling, but it's wrong. The ceiling looks like it's only three feet from my face instead of seven. I'm thinking, *why is it so close?* Then I look to my right, and I can see completely into the front yard through the window. Normally from the couch, I can only see the upper third of that window—just trees and sky. But I could see the whole yard. That's when I realized: I'm floating. I'm off the couch."

The out-of-body experience might have been dismissed as sleep paralysis or a vivid dream, except for what happened next.

"My whole body felt like it was buzzing, vibrating. My vision was a little distorted, maybe because I'd fallen asleep with my contacts in, but then I saw it. In my front yard, there's this small gray figure. Classic gray alien appearance—large head, big black eyes, thin body. It's just standing there in my yard, looking at the house. Looking at me."

The terror in Hunter's voice was palpable even in the retelling. This wasn't a vague shadow or a might-have-been. This was a clear, distinct entity standing in his front yard while he floated helplessly above his couch.

"Did it seem threatening?" Ward asked.

Hunter considered. "I didn't have time to really decide. My first instinct wasn't that it was threatening, more like…it was observing. Like it was studying me or waiting for something. But the whole situation was wrong. I'm floating above my couch, looking at this thing that shouldn't exist, and I remember what Tony told me—if something like this happens again, call on the name of Jesus.

"The moment I said 'Jesus,' it was violent. Not the gray thing doing something violent, but my return to my body. It wasn't like gently floating down—I was slammed back into myself. Like being thrown back into my body with force."

The experience left Hunter shaken for days. His wife had noticed his distress but struggled to understand what he'd experienced. How do you explain to someone that you floated out of your body and saw an alien in your yard? How do you process that as reality when everything in our culture says it's impossible?

THE ESCALATION PATTERN

Hunter's progression from occasional sleep paralysis in 2015 to weekly interdimensional encounters by 2023 revealed a deliberate escalation pattern. The entities—whatever they were—had been slowly increasing their presence in his life, testing boundaries, establishing connection.

"It started maybe once a year," Hunter explained. "Then once a quarter. Then monthly. Now it's weekly. And each time, the experiences get more intense, more physical."

This gradual escalation appears in many abduction and interdimensional contact cases. The entities seem to acclimate their subjects slowly, building tolerance to the experiences like someone might build tolerance to a drug. By the time the encounters become overtly physical or threatening, the experiencer has been conditioned to accept them as part of reality.

But Hunter's case had an additional element: the correlation with his heart rate. His Apple Watch data showed that experiences intensified when his heart rate dropped below 35 beats per minute. On the night of the gray encounter, his heart rate had been in the low 30s for over an hour.

"I think my body naturally does what other people try to achieve through meditation or drugs," Hunter said. "It's like I involuntarily slip into this state where the veil is thinner."

HUMAN AGENTS IN SPIRITUAL WARFARE

The hooded figures in Hunter's vision represented a crucial revelation: the spiritual warfare I was experiencing involved human agents. These weren't just demons or interdimensional entities—these were people who had aligned themselves with dark forces.

Throughout Scripture, we see examples of humans who served as agents of spiritual darkness. The witch of Endor, who summoned Samuel's spirit for King Saul, demonstrated that some humans could manipulate spiritual realms through forbidden practices. Simon the Sorcerer in Acts 8 had used sorcery to bewitch the people of Samaria, wielding genuine supernatural power before his encounter with Philip.

Elymas the sorcerer actively opposed Paul's ministry in Acts 13, trying to turn the proconsul away from faith. Paul, filled with the Holy Spirit, recognized him for what he was: *"O full of all subtilty and all mischief, thou child of the devil, thou enemy of all righteousness, wilt thou not cease to pervert the right ways of the Lord?"* (Acts 13:10 KJV).

These biblical examples show that human agents of darkness are not merely deceived individuals but active participants in spiritual warfare. They make conscious choices to align with dark forces, gaining certain powers in exchange for their service.

The druids following me into my house represented this same dynamic in modern form. Pastor Dave Bryan's immediate identification of them as "druids" and "witches" wasn't speculation—it was recognition. He'd encountered such beings before, understood their methods and purposes.

"The hooded cloaks are ceremonial," Pastor Bryan had explained. "It's how they appear when they're operating in the spiritual realm. They may look completely normal in the physical world—your neighbor, someone at the grocery store—but in the spirit, their true nature is revealed."

This revelation fundamentally changed how I understood the opposition. It wasn't enough to pray against spiritual forces. There were actual people, possibly in my community, who had dedicated themselves to opposing my ministry through occult means.

THE TECHNOLOGY OF CONTACT

The windmill sound that preceded Hunter's experiences connected to a broader pattern I'd documented across hundreds of episodes. At least three other witnesses had described identical sounds before their own interdimensional encounters. But Hunter's description added new details that suggested a technological component to these experiences.

"It's not just the sound," Hunter explained. "My whole body vibrates at a specific frequency. It's like every cell is resonating. And right before something happens, there's this electrical feeling in the air, like right before lightning strikes."

This description aligns with theoretical physics models of dimensional travel. If entities were moving between dimensions, they would need to match the vibrational frequency of our reality. The sound might be a by-product of that synchronization—the auditory signature of a portal opening or a dimensional barrier being breached.

Hunter had inadvertently tested this theory when, inspired by a *Blurry Creatures* podcast episode about UFO highway phenomena, he attempted to film UFOs using his phone's slow-motion feature. The podcast had suggested that UFOs move too fast for normal vision but can be captured in slow-motion video.

"I go outside with my phone, ready to use slow-mo," Hunter recounted. "But before I even switched to slow-motion mode, two craft appeared over my house. Clear as day. Not planes, not helicopters—something else entirely. They moved in ways that violated physics as I understand it. It felt like I knocked on a door and they answered," Hunter said. "Three days later, the gray showed up."

This suggested intentionality and awareness. The entities knew Hunter was looking for them. They responded to his attention, even his intention, before he'd taken any physical action. This level of awareness and response indicated intelligence, planning, and possibly surveillance.

THE RH-NEGATIVE FACTOR AND BIBLICAL BLOODLINES

As cited previously, Hunter's Rh-negative blood type added another layer to the mystery. This rare blood type, present in only 15 percent of the global population, appears in nearly 90 percent of people reporting interdimensional experiences. The correlation is too strong to be a coincidence.

Cameraman Joel's research had uncovered disturbing connections between Rh-negative blood and the biblical Nephilim. "In Genesis 6, we read about the sons of God taking human wives and producing offspring," Joel explained. "These Nephilim were hybrids—part human, part something else. The text says 'There were giants in the earth in those days; and also after that,' suggesting these bloodlines continued after the flood."

The book of Enoch, while not canonical, provides additional detail about these hybrid beings. It describes how they possessed knowledge and abilities that violated natural order—they could manipulate both physical and spiritual realms, see into multiple dimensions, and exercise powers that normal humans couldn't access.

"What if Rh-negative blood is a genetic marker from those pre-flood bloodlines?" Joel proposed. "It would explain why these individuals have such high rates of supernatural experiences. They're literally built differently at a genetic level."

Hunter's family history supported this theory. His mother, also likely Rh-negative, had experienced supernatural phenomena throughout her life. She could see and hear things in their haunted childhood home that Hunter's father remained completely blind to. The sensitivity ran in family lines, passed down through blood like an ancient inheritance.

As previously mentioned, in the Basque region of Spain and France, where Rh-negative blood appears as high as approximately 35 percent of the population—far above the global average—the people speak Euskera, a language that predates all other European languages and has no known linguistic relatives. Linguists can't trace its origins or connect it to any other language family. Could this be a remnant of pre-Babel speech, preserved in a population that carries these ancient genetic markers?

The implications were staggering. If certain bloodlines carried enhanced spiritual sensitivity from the Nephilim era, it would explain why certain families experienced generational hauntings, why some people could see into the spiritual realm from childhood, and why entities seemed to target specific genetic lines across multiple generations.

THE PROPHETIC BURDEN

As our studio session continued, the weight of Hunter's revelations pressed down on all of us. Jack, unable to speak without a microphone, was furiously texting questions to me. Ward was connecting patterns to his own research into supernatural phenomena. Joel was diving deeper into the bloodline implications.

But I was grappling with the personal nature of the prophecy. Hunter had seen my house, described it perfectly, and witnessed spiritual enemies following me into my sanctuary. This wasn't abstract spiritual warfare—it was specific, targeted, and immediate.

"Do you understand what this means for me?" I asked Hunter. "You're telling me that right now, there are entities—human and otherwise—that have marked me, that know where I live, that are actively working against me."

Hunter nodded slowly. "That's why I had to come. That's why I drove three and a half hours despite being exhausted. You needed to know. God wanted you to know."

The parallel to biblical prophets was unmistakable. They rarely wanted their gift. Jeremiah wept over his prophecies. Jonah ran from his calling. Daniel became physically ill from his visions. The burden of seeing into the spiritual realm, of carrying divine warnings to others, was never portrayed as a blessing in Scripture—it was a responsibility, often a terrible one.

Hunter carried that same burden. He didn't ask for these experiences, didn't seek out the ability to remote view or travel interdimensionally. But God had allowed—perhaps ordained—his sensitivity for purposes like this: to warn a fellow believer of danger.

THE COORDINATION OF OPPOSITION

What struck me most about Hunter's revelation was how it revealed the coordination between different types of opposition. The dogman that had attacked him in dreams and appeared in physical form. The gray entities conducting surveillance. The human druids following me. These weren't random, disconnected events—they were coordinated activities by forces aligned against God's Kingdom.

This coordination appears in Revelation's description of the end times, where the dragon, beast, and false prophet work together despite being distinct entities. Each has its own role, its own methods, but they serve the same ultimate purpose: opposition to God and His people.

Hunter's experiences revealed this same pattern in microcosm:

- Physical creatures (dogmen) creating fear and trauma.
- Technological/interdimensional entities (grays) conducting surveillance and possibly experimentation.
- Human agents (druids) performing targeted spiritual attacks.
- All working together to discourage, distract, or destroy those serving God's purposes.

The sophistication of this coordinated assault suggested organization beyond what random demonic harassment would produce. There was strategy here, planning, and resource allocation. Different types of entities are deployed for different purposes, all serving a unified agenda.

THE DEFENSE OF THE DIVINE NAME

Throughout all of Hunter's experiences, one defense proved consistently effective: the name of Jesus. Whether facing the dogman in the woods, floating out of his body with a gray entity watching, or experiencing the weekly intrusions preceded by the windmill sound—calling on Christ's name ended the experience immediately.

"It's not like it gradually fades," Hunter emphasized. "The second I say 'Jesus,' it's over. Boom. Instant."

This immediate response aligned with Paul's declaration: *"That at the name of Jesus every knee should bow, of things in heaven, and things in earth, and things under the earth"* (Philippians 2:10 KJV). The entities—regardless of their type or origin—remain subject to Christ's authority.

But Hunter had learned there was a difference between using Jesus's name as a spiritual panic button and walking in a continuous relationship with Christ. "I'm trying to pray more consistently," he explained. "Not just when something scary happens, but throughout the day. Building that protection before the attacks come."

This proactive spiritual discipline reflected biblical wisdom. Paul instructed believers to *"Pray without ceasing"* (1 Thessalonians 5:17 KJV) and to *"Put on the whole armour of God, that ye may be able to stand against the wiles of the devil"* (Ephesians 6:11 KJV). The armor wasn't meant to be grabbed in the moment of attack—it was meant to be worn continuously.

THE GENERATIONAL IMPACT

Perhaps the most sobering aspect of Hunter's story was its impact on his children, particularly his 11-year-old son who had witnessed the dogman in the woods. The boy had seen something that violated everything he'd been taught about reality. How does a child process such knowledge?

"He remembers everything," Hunter said quietly. "But he doesn't want to talk about it. Sometimes I'll carefully bring it up, just to check in, and he'll acknowledge it happened but then change the subject."

This response—acknowledgment without discussion—is common among young witnesses to supernatural events. The experience is too real to deny but too disturbing to dwell on. Many children who encounter such phenomena develop a kind of compartmentalization, keeping the supernatural experience separate from their daily life as a psychological protection mechanism.

But the experience had marked the boy, initiated him into a reality that most people can comfortably deny. He now knows that monsters are real, that they could step out of nightmares into the waking world, that his father's protection had limits against certain threats.

This generational transmission of spiritual sensitivity appears throughout Scripture. Samuel was dedicated to God's service from birth. Jeremiah was told, *"Before I formed you in the womb I knew you, before you were born I set you apart; I appointed you as a prophet to the nations"* (Jeremiah 1:5 NIV). Some people are marked from birth for spiritual sight, for better or worse.

THE MINISTRY UNDER SIEGE

As Hunter shared his prophecy, I couldn't help but reflect on the past 18 months of preparation I've been sensing. The feeling had started as a whisper, a gentle prompting to deepen my prayer life, to study spiritual warfare, to prepare for something coming. Over time, it had intensified to a clear impression: a major spiritual battle was approaching.

"I've been feeling this for over a year," I told Hunter and the team. "But part of me wondered if I was just being dramatic, reading into things because of what I do for a living. Your vision eliminates that doubt."

The druids following me into my house proved that the enemy had already deployed assets. This wasn't future tense—it was present reality. The war wasn't coming; it was here.

The implications for my ministry were sobering. Every episode of *The Confessionals* that exposed the enemy's operations, every testimony that revealed the reality of spiritual warfare, every person who found faith or renewed their faith through the show—all of it made me a target. The more effective the ministry, the more intense the opposition.

But God, in His sovereignty, had arranged for Hunter to see it. He had pulled back the veil not to terrify but to prepare. The warning was an act of divine mercy, giving me time to strengthen my defenses, to prepare my family, to rally prayer support.

THE COMMISSION CONFIRMED

As Hunter prepared to leave the studio, driving back into the Tennessee night, the full weight of what had transpired settled over us. He had delivered a prophetic warning that would fundamentally change how I approached my life and ministry. He had confirmed that the spiritual warfare I'd been sensing was real, immediate, and involved both human and nonhuman opposition.

But more than that, Hunter's journey from dogman encounter to prophetic messenger illustrated how God repurposes what the enemy means for evil. The same sensitivity that made Hunter vulnerable to interdimensional attack also made him capable of receiving prophetic dreams. The same bloodline that attracted entity attention also carried the capacity for supernatural discernment.

"I almost didn't come today," Hunter admitted as he gathered his things. "Last night I was so tired, I thought about canceling. But when I woke up this morning, I knew I had to be here. There was no question."

Divine appointments rarely arrive at convenient times. God's timing supersedes human comfort, human logic, and human convenience. Hunter had driven four hours on little sleep, after a 60-hour work week, to deliver a message that I desperately needed to hear.

As I watched his truck disappear down the dark road, I understood that we were all part of something larger than our individual experiences. The dogmen, the grays, the druids, the prophetic dreams—they were all pieces of an interdimensional chess game playing out across multiple realms simultaneously.

But we weren't pawns. We were warriors, equipped with authority in Christ that transcended dimensional boundaries. The entities knew it. The druids knew it. And now, thanks to Hunter's courage in sharing his vision, I knew it too.

The veil had spoken, revealing both the danger and the divine protection surrounding those who serve God's purposes. The dreams that reveal dangers also reveal deliverers. The veil that allows enemies to cross also allows angels to minister. And sometimes, God sends a tired contractor from Middle Tennessee to warn a podcaster in East Tennessee that the battle he's been sensing is more real than he ever imagined.

THE BROADER PATTERN EMERGES

Hunter's revelation about the druids following me into my home had shaken me to my core. But it was only the beginning of understanding the scope of human involvement in the spiritual war surrounding *The Confessionals.*

For weeks after Hunter's visit, I couldn't shake his words about human agents operating in the spiritual realm. Druids. Witches. People who looked normal in everyday life but served dark masters through occult practices. The idea that actual humans were actively working against my ministry—not just spiritual entities but flesh-and-blood people performing rituals and ceremonies—fundamentally changed how I understood the opposition.

I began researching, diving into the history and practices of modern druidism and occultism. What I discovered was a vast network of organized groups, some operating openly, others in carefully guarded secrecy. These weren't just misguided individuals playing with tarot cards or burning sage. These were coordinated organizations with hierarchies, funding, and specific methodologies for opening doorways between dimensions.

Then, in early 2023, an email arrived that would confirm everything Hunter had warned about—and reveal depths of human involvement in supernatural manifestation I hadn't imagined possible.

The testimony came from a man named James who'd narrowly escaped what he described as a "portal ritual" in Joshua Tree. As I read his account, the pieces began connecting. The druids Hunter had seen weren't isolated actors. They were part of a massive, organized system where human agents deliberately tear open the fabric between dimensions, using everything from ancient ritual practices to modern frequency technology.

James's story would reveal not just the existence of these groups, but their methods—how they target victims, how they manipulate consciousness through sound, and most disturbingly, how they succeed in manifesting visible portals between our world and theirs.

What Hunter had seen prophetically, James had experienced physically. The human agents weren't just following and observing—they were actively working to bridge hell and earth. And they were getting better at it.

10

The Desert Portal

When Human Agents Open the Gates

Have nothing to do with the fruitless deeds of darkness, but rather expose them. It is shameful even to mention what the disobedient do in secret.

—Ephesians 5:11-12 NIV

The text message changed everything. "There's a party in Joshua Tree—you have to come."

James had no idea that accepting this invitation would thrust him into a carefully orchestrated supernatural trap, one that would reveal how human agents deliberately tear open the fabric between dimensions to manifest evil in our world. His testimony, corroborated by former satanic high wizard Zachary King, exposes the terrifying reality that organized occult groups actively work to bridge the gap between hell and earth—and they're getting better at it.

THE ARCHITECTURE OF DECEPTION

James's targeting began not in the desert, but in a Hollywood bar where coincidences don't exist. The man who approached him—let's call him Mark—wasn't making casual conversation. He was hunting.

"Looking back, every red flag was there," James told me during our three-hour interview. "He bought me drinks within minutes of meeting me. He knew exactly which buttons to push. When my friend left, uncomfortable with the gothic bar Mark led us to, I should have left too. But I was curious."

Curiosity—satan's favorite bait since Eden.

The gothic bar with its "really sketchy" atmosphere wasn't just Mark's preferred hangout. It was a filtering mechanism. James's friend Daniel fled immediately, his spiritual discernment intact. But James stayed, passing the first test: he could tolerate darkness.

"How do you know I'm not trying to kill you?" Mark asked during their drive to Joshua Tree a question so bizarre that James initially laughed it off. But this wasn't dark humor—it was spiritual reconnaissance. Mark was gauging James's awareness level, testing how much he could perceive about the danger he was in.

When Zachary King heard this part of the story, his response was immediate: "The VIPs are your new victims. You're going to initiate them in some way, and hopefully they'll want to play. He apparently did not want to play."

THE RITUAL PREPARATION

The party location itself was no accident. Set in a natural canyon in Joshua Tree in California, the geography created what occultists call a "cauldron"—a contained space where spiritual energy can be concentrated and controlled. James arrived at dawn on Saturday, April 2, 2022, exhausted and disoriented from the overnight drive. This, too, was intentional.

"Sleep deprivation makes you more susceptible," King explained. "Your natural defenses are down. Your discernment is compromised. It's why a lot of these events happen at night or after keeping people awake for extended periods."

During daylight hours, the gathering appeared almost mundane—perhaps a hundred people, RVs, tents, the atmosphere of a desert rave. But James noticed oddities that shouldn't have been there. When asked if he was Jewish, the question came with an undercurrent of menace. When he mentioned his Catholic upbringing, Mark pulled him aside urgently: "You're saying too much right now. Don't be telling people that stuff."

> *Be sober, be vigilant; because your adversary the devil, as a roaring lion, walketh about, seeking whom he may devour* (1 Peter 5:8 KJV).

The VIP bracelet James received from a man in a Mad Hatter hat marked him as special—but not in the way he assumed. When I showed him a screenshot from Pink's music video featuring a high wizard in similar attire, James confirmed: "During the day he had less face paint, but at night, he looked just like that."

King's explanation chilled me: "When they give those bracelets out, the VIPs are their new victims. They are going to be initiated in some way."

THE SONIC ARCHITECTURE OF EVIL

What James didn't understand at the time was that the twin DJs who arrived weren't just providing entertainment—they were sonic engineers in a spiritual war that traces back decades. Dr. Laura Sanger has been a guest on my podcast, and her research reveals that since the 1930s, the Rothschild-Rockefeller alliance has funded scientific studies examining how musical frequencies could prepare the masses for war and create mass hysteria.

"The Rockefeller Foundation archives showed their research focused on psychotronic warfare, physiological stress induction, negative affective emotional arousal, mass persuasion, herd behavior, and population control," Sanger discovered. "People's bodies would bioenergetically entrain to the musical frequencies and electronically engineered sound effects."

This wasn't conspiracy theory—it was documented history. According to researchers like Dr. Leonard Horowitz, in 1939, Nazi propagandist Joseph Goebbels, funded by the same alliance, organized a conference in London that changed the standard tuning of A from 435 Hz to 440 Hz. The timing—just months before World War II—was no coincidence.

The 440 Hz frequency is destructive, creating disharmonious resonance in the brain that can lead to disease and war. Recent studies confirm this: water fleas exposed to 440 Hz developed infertility and decreased heart rates, eventually dying weeks after exposure. Humans exposed to the same frequency showed increased negative emotions, particularly in men—perfect for stirring the rage necessary for conflict.

As Shane Lynch of Boyzone revealed in a 2023 podcast interview with me: "I've been in rooms at the top of the top where albums are prayed over demonically. Music is prayed over demonically. That goes out to the radio stations, to the public. When you see that stuff, it's frightening.... It's a satanic music industry."

THE TRANSFORMATION HOUR

As darkness fell on Saturday night, April 2 became April 3—a date that appears in declassified government documents as "unholy blood falls," designated for "human sacrifice, male, female, or child, any age."

The transformation was systematic and deliberate. The twins' music began—but this wasn't entertainment. They were weaponizing frequency itself, employing what Harold Burris Meyer pioneered in 1938: sound technology designed to control emotional responses and create mass hysteria.

"I saw everyone's clothing change," James reported. "People who'd been wearing normal clothes were suddenly in black robes, soaking wet-looking. Faces began shape-shifting. Yellow eyes appeared. What looked like vampires emerged from nowhere."

King confirmed these manifestations are standard at high-level rituals: "People with yellow eyes, you see that at satanic events. People that you think are vampires, good chance they are."

But there was more happening than visual transformation. The electronic music operated at specific frequencies designed to alter brainwave patterns, creating what researchers call "frequency following response"—the tendency of brainwaves to synchronize with external rhythms. The human body, composed of 60-70 percent water, was literally being restructured at the molecular level by these sonic weapons.

Dr. Laura Sanger's research into Masaru Emoto's work proves this isn't metaphor—water molecules physically change structure based on the frequencies they receive. Positive messages create beautiful, perfect crystals; negative ones produce ugly, chaotic formations. The bodies at that ritual were being systematically corrupted at the cellular level.

THE PORTAL MANIFESTATION

The climactic moment defied natural law but followed both supernatural and scientific precedent. James watched in horror as the DJ tent lifted into the air, revealing a swirling green portal beneath. People began flying—not metaphorically, but literally ascending into the vortex while screaming in unison at an ear-piercing frequency.

That unified scream wasn't random—it was a frequency key. Andrea Rynberk, who works with survivors of satanic ritual abuse, explained to Dr. Sanger that "frequencies open portals. The more intense the emotions stirred up in a child, the lower the resonance. At extreme levels of torture, portals are actually opened up for deceased Nephilim to come into our dimension."

When I expressed skepticism about people actually flying, King's response stunned me: "I levitated, and I went up about 300 feet. Demons lift you up, demons levitate you. You look like you have all these amazing powers, and you don't. It's just a demon doing it."

The portal itself fits patterns observed throughout occult history. As Sanger notes during her interview with me, these frequencies have been "weaponized to torture and program people enslaved in satanic ritual abuse." The survivors she works with confirm that specific frequencies are trained into certain parts of the brain to respond to certain sounds—often subliminally.

THE HYPNOTIC CONTROL SYSTEM

What James experienced mirrors what happened in ancient Babylon under Nebuchadnezzar, when music was first weaponized for mass mind control. As Daniel 3:4-7 records, specific instruments playing together created a hypnotic effect that caused entire populations to bow before golden idols. Only those who maintained spiritual purity—Shadrach, Meshach, and Abednego—could resist the entrainment.

The band Foremost Poets exposed this agenda in their 1999 song "Moonraker," with lyrics that read like a confession: "An unidentified frequency has been existing in the system for some time.... This frequency has been used by a secret society in conjunction with Lucifer to lure and prey on innocent party goers with hypnotism, syncroprism, technology, lies, scandal, and pornography."[1]

Professor Douglas Fields from the University of Maryland confirmed the science in 2012: "When people move in synchrony, they're more likely to perceive the world in synchrony...that would facilitate their ability to interact." In other words, group dancing at concerts creates programmable herd consciousness.

THE TECHNOLOGY OF SUMMONING

The methodology employed that night represented centuries of refined occult practice enhanced by modern understanding. The location, the date, the music frequencies, the sleep deprivation, the chemical alterations (James suspected drugs were added to his drinks), and the collective ritualistic focus—all designed to achieve what King calls "dimensional synchronization."

"It's not random," Zachary King emphasized. "These events happen at the same place, at the same time every year. You have to book the high wizard to be there. It costs a lot of money."

But now they had something their predecessors lacked: electronic enhancement. Modern occultists employ:

- Frequency generators producing specific brainwave entrainment patterns.
- Electromagnetic field manipulators affecting consciousness.
- Coordinated smartphone apps synchronizing global ritual participation.
- Social media platforms for instant recruitment and screening.
- Digital currencies for untraceable funding.

The 440 Hz standard tuning ensured every piece of music played that night was already priming consciousness for darkness. Combined with the specific ritual frequencies, the desert's natural electromagnetic properties, and concentrated spiritual energy, optimal conditions for dimensional breach were achieved.

James's phone malfunctioning—stuck at 11:11, unable to record—wasn't random. These frequencies generate electromagnetic anomalies that affect electronic devices, documented across hundreds of supernatural encounters.

THE HUMAN INFRASTRUCTURE OF EVIL

Perhaps most disturbing was the revelation that this wasn't a one-time event but part of an established network. When

James escaped and made it to a hospital, refusing their offers to call the police, he understood instinctively that human authorities couldn't address what had happened to him. The infrastructure supporting these rituals extends into legitimate institutions.

Military personnel from the nearby 29 Palms base confirmed to me that they witnessed identical gatherings at the same coordinates. The location operates year after year, protected by both supernatural and human forces.

"Your danger is that there's going to be territorial demons that stake the place out," King warned when I mentioned plans to investigate the site. "They'll know if you're there. Whether you see anything or get killed will be up to them."

THE ESCAPE PROTOCOL

James's survival depended on one thing: invoking the name of Jesus Christ. As he ran through the desert, cloaked figures pursuing him, he encountered resistance that had nothing to do with physical exhaustion.

"It felt like I was pushing through something invisible," he said. "Like the air itself was thick, holding me back. I couldn't move forward until I started crying out 'Jesus guides me, I walk with Jesus.' Every time I said it, it got easier to move."

> *That at the name of Jesus every knee should bow, of things in heaven, and things in earth, and things under the earth* (Philippians 2:10 KJV).

The force field James encountered represents what occultists call a "ritual boundary"—a demonically maintained perimeter designed to contain the spiritual energy and prevent victims from escaping. But there's more: it was held in place by frequency. The unified screaming, the electronic music, the ritual chanting—all created a sonic prison.

During our interview, Dr. Sanger revealed the escape: "Genuine worship in spirit and truth actually cancels out harmful frequencies meant to destroy us." James's desperate cries to Jesus weren't just prayers—they were counter-frequencies, divine sound waves breaking satanic sonic bondage.

BREAKING THE SONIC SPELL

The systematic nature of James's recruitment followed protocols King knew well, but with a modern twist. Today's occultists understand what the Rockefeller Foundation discovered decades ago: you can program humans through frequency. Every bar James visited, every song played in Mark's car, every moment leading to that desert gathering was orchestrated with specific frequencies designed to lower his resistance.

But God's counter-frequency system predates all satanic perversion. As Sanger discovered, when creation was spoken into existence, 528 Hz was key in sustaining life. The sun vibrates at 528 Hz. Chlorophyll, which converts sunlight to oxygen, resonates at 528 Hz. This "miracle tone" is the frequency scientists use to repair DNA.

The standard tuning of A to 444 Hz (not the destructive 440 Hz) aligns with these divine frequencies. When instruments are tuned to 444 Hz, playing certain notes produces the exact Solfeggio frequencies used for healing. It's what David likely used when his harp drove demons from King Saul—the original sonic warfare turned to divine purpose. (See 1 Samuel 16:23.)

THE ACCELERATION OF MANIFESTATION

What James witnessed represents an escalation in boldness and capability. Where once these groups operated in absolute secrecy, they now hold events with hundreds of participants. Where once manifestations were subtle, they now include visible portals and mass levitation.

"Satan hides in plain sight," King observed. "In the last few years, we've had multiple Satan Cons, public black masses, and the Satanic Temple declaring abortion as a sacrament. They're not hiding anymore because they don't have to."

The membership numbers confirm this acceleration. The Satanic Temple grew from 300,000 to 700,000 members in a single year. Marina Abramović openly practices "spirit cooking" while being appointed to rebuild Ukraine's education system.[2] The same celebrities attending her rituals appear at gatherings like the one James experienced.

But most alarming is the sonic infiltration of everyday life. Every song on the radio, every streaming service, every concert venue—all standardized to 440 Hz, all priming human consciousness for manipulation. As Dr. Leonard Horowitz concluded: "The intensive research into the military and commercial value of compelling herd behavior with music to induce stress, promote diseases, and suppress spirituality has enabled the world's wealthiest people to exercise cultural control through programming."[3]

THE DIVINE RESPONSE

Yet even in this darkness, God's sovereignty remains absolute. James survived because prayer still works. The name of

Jesus still carries authority. The blood of Christ still provides protection.

But there's more we can do. As Dr. Laura Sanger reveals: "When we read the Word of God out loud, imagine what it's doing to our cells." The Word isn't just spiritual—it's sonic. Every Scripture spoken aloud creates frequencies that restructure our very molecules toward divine order.

> *So is my word that goes out from my mouth: It will not return to me empty, but will accomplish what I desire and achieve the purpose for which I sent it* (Isaiah 55:11 NIV).

When King left satanism after encountering a "blessed Miraculous Medal," he discovered the truth that terrifies every occultist: "I knew beyond a shadow of a doubt I had not sold my soul to the devil when I was 13. I knew that Jesus Christ was my Lord and Savior. I knew that all my magic, my occult, my satanism and my New Age were all fake—one big pile of crap."

THE CALL TO SONIC SPIRITUAL WARFARE

James's testimony, verified by multiple witnesses and corroborated by both King's inside knowledge and Sanger's frequency research, demands a response. We cannot remain passive while human agents actively work to manifest hell on earth through sonic warfare.

The location James escaped from continues operating. The people who targeted him remain free. The infrastructure supporting these rituals grows stronger each year. And most Christians remain blissfully unaware that they're being bombarded with destructive frequencies every moment of every day.

> *Put on the full armor of God, so that you can take your stand against the devil's schemes. For our struggle is not against flesh and blood, but against the rulers, against the authorities, against the powers of this dark world and against the spiritual forces of evil in the heavenly realms* (Ephesians 6:11-12 NIV).

But now we know their weapons. We know their frequencies. And we know the counter-frequencies of Heaven. If we combine the Word of God with worship in spirit and truth, tuned to divine frequencies, no sonic weapon formed against us will prosper.

The evidence is clear: Human agents, working with demonic forces, regularly open portals between dimensions using weaponized sound. They target victims systematically. They operate with impunity. And they're not stopping.

The question isn't whether this is happening—James's testimony, King's confirmation, and Sanger's research remove all doubt. The question is: What frequency will you choose to resonate with?

If human beings can dedicate themselves so completely to evil that they manifest literal portals to hell through corrupted sound, how much more should Christians dedicate themselves to releasing Heaven's frequencies on earth? If satanists gather by the hundreds for their sonic rituals, where are the hundreds of Christians gathering to release divine sound?

The desert portal remains active. The next gathering is already being planned. The frequencies are already being prepared. And somewhere, another James is being targeted, unaware of the supernatural sonic trap being set.

But now you know. You know about the 440 Hz deception. You know about frequency weapons. You know about sonic portals. And you know the power of divine counter-frequencies.

The question is: Will you act on this knowledge, or will you dismiss it as too extreme, too uncomfortable, too demanding of response?

The choice, like James's that night in the desert, is yours. But remember—in this spiritual war, neutrality is not an option. Every frequency you absorb, every song you hear, every sound that enters your being is either aligning you with Heaven or entraining you toward hell.

The demons know this. The occultists know this. The Rockefellers and Rothschilds have known it for nearly a century.

Now you know it too.

NOTES

1 Foremost Poets, "Moonraker Lyrics"; https://www.justsomelyrics.com/2381086/foremost-poets-moonraker-lyrics.html.

2 Mayank Kasyap, "Who is Marina Abramovic? Ukraine's Ambassador Linked To 'Spirit Cooking,'" News24Online.com, September 23, 2023; https://news24online.com/world/who-is-marina-abramovic-ukraines-ambassador-linked-to-spirit-cooking-mkir/173810/.

3 Dr. Leonard Horowitz, "Musical Cult Control: The Rockefeller Foundation's War on Consciousness Through the Imposition of A=440 hz Standard Tuning," Soundquality.org, nd.; https://soundquality.org/wp-content/uploads/2023/03/musical_cult_control_horowitz.pdf.

11

The Dark Shift

When Humans Cross Over

For we wrestle not against flesh and blood, but against principalities, against powers, against the rulers of the darkness of this world, against spiritual wickedness in high places.

—Ephesians 6:12 KJV

James ran through the desert calling on the name of Jesus while a portal swirled behind him. Human agents had orchestrated the whole thing—the recruitment, the frequencies, the ritual. But what kept nagging at me after his testimony wasn't the portal itself. It was the people. The human beings who had willingly aligned themselves with darkness, who had learned to manipulate spiritual forces like tools in a toolbox.

I kept asking myself: how deep does that go? How organized is the human side of this war? James showed me that people can open doors between dimensions. Hunter showed me that human agents—druids, witches—were following me into my own home. But I hadn't yet encountered someone who could walk through those doors themselves. Someone whose body had been so entangled with the other side that the boundary between human and entity had started to blur.

Then Russ called.

THE PURSUIT THAT CHANGED EVERYTHING

The light in the sky pulsed like a heartbeat, maintaining perfect distance as Russ and his friend Ron chased it through wet roads.

"It looked like stadium lights," Russ explained, describing that night in 2014 when curiosity nearly cost him everything. He and Ron had just finished a shift at the restaurant where they worked. It was around two in the morning. Ron had stepped out for a cigarette, and Russ, looking up over the hill behind his porch, noticed a whitish pulsing light in the sky—bigger than it should have been if it was from the nearby baseball field, and it wasn't moving.

Russ had no idea that pursuing that unexplained light would thrust him into a world where humans routinely pierce the veil between dimensions, where entities recruit children through dreams, and where some people become so entangled with the other side that their bodies *physically transform* to accommodate visitors from another realm.

I sat down with Russ for the first time in November 2021, and he gave me one of the wildest accounts I've ever heard. Usually, I don't have threads to pull at after an interview. But after my interview with Russ, I had threads everywhere. And for the next three years, I pulled at them.

His testimony, corroborated by multiple witnesses including his own brother, exposes what appears to be a systematic program of interdimensional recruitment that targets specific bloodlines and abilities. What emerges isn't random paranormal activity—it's organized, hierarchical, and disturbingly purposeful.

Not every claim in what follows can be independently verified. A lot of what I'm about to share comes from Ron, filtered through Russ's memory of conversations that unfolded in fragments over years. But the consistency of what I was able to confirm, combined with the way this testimony lines up with patterns I've documented across hundreds of other episodes, made me certain this story needed to be told.

With the strange bright light still in the sky, Russ and Ron got in Ron's car to check it out. The spot Russ thought the light was coming from was 30 seconds from his house. He didn't grab shoes, didn't bring a phone. They drove to where the light should have been, yet nothing was there. But the light itself stayed the same distance away, pulsing steadily in the clouds.

So they kept following it.

> *Be sober, be vigilant; because your adversary the devil, as a roaring lion, walketh about, seeking whom he may devour* (1 Peter 5:8 KJV).

The chase led them out of the city and into farmland. They stopped on a county road and got out to look. The light was still there, same distance, same pulsing rhythm. Then from the far side of an empty crop field came a sound like hyenas—or something trying to sound like hyenas. It scared both of them back into the car. But instead of turning around, they kept chasing.

Everywhere they drove, the ground was wet. It wasn't raining. It hadn't rained. But the route they were taking was always wet. Russ noticed this detail and couldn't explain it.

About 20 minutes outside the city, they stopped again on a county road that pointed straight at the light. This time it was closer than before. Just a little. But enough to feel different. Russ turned to look at Ron, and everything about his friend had changed. Ron—normally jokey, always talking—was staring at the light with a focus that made Russ's skin crawl.

Then Ron said, "Get back in the [expletive] car. We're going right now."

Ron spun the car around and floored it. He was white-knuckling the steering wheel, hunched forward, checking the rear-view mirror over and over. The light was following them, and it was gaining a little. Ron started muttering, "How's it here? I don't know why he's here. I'm sorry. I'm sorry."

Russ was spiraling into panic. He kept asking what was happening, and Ron gave him fragments of a bizarre story between mirror checks. This thing was an entity from someplace else. Ron had worked for it for years. It wasn't supposed to be able to come to our side. But it was here now, and it had found him.

Russ thought Ron was playing a joke on him. He begged him to stop. Instead, Ron said, "Call my girlfriend. She'll back it all up."

So Russ called her. When she answered, all he said to her was, "Is what he's saying true?" He didn't give her any details, didn't say what Ron had told him. And she replied, "Oh, the thing"—and she used the entity's name without being prompted. *"Sujent."* Then she said, "Yeah, that's all true. Do what he says. He'll make sure you're safe."

That 45-minute chase over wet Indiana roads ended when the light stopped following them a couple minutes before they reached Russ's house. He didn't notice until they were already there, and the light was suddenly gone. But the night wasn't over.

WHAT HAPPENED AT THE HOUSE

They pulled into Russ's driveway. Ron's girlfriend met them there. Ron said, "I'll be back," and took off running up the steep hill next to the house—fast. Exceptionally fast. Faster than a normal person should be able to move.

The route Ron took—up one steep hill, around an entire city block, down an alley—should have taken several minutes. Russ described the street next to his house as "crazy steep—like a [expletive] mountain." Ron covered all of it in seconds.

Then from the alley behind the house came an unreal sound—like something got ripped apart. Like an animal was just destroyed. And Ron walked out of the darkness, covered in patches of something dark. Russ remembers it as possibly greenish, possibly black, but it looked like blood. Dark blood, all over his arms and shirt.

Ron emerged exhausted. He told Russ the thing he'd just killed was stationed there—sent by the entity, put there to watch Russ or his brother, maybe to act if the timing was right. Later, much later, Ron would describe whatever he'd destroyed as looking like "black licorice." (That's how Russ described it to me, and I remember thinking, *That description is so bizarre that no one would make that up.)*

Ron and his girlfriend got in their car and drove home. Russ stood in his driveway, alone, staring at the sky where the light had been. Then he got in his car and drove to his girlfriend's house. She was asleep. He crawled in beside her, and when she asked if he was okay, all he said was, "I just really want to be here right now."

He stared at the ceiling for hours.

THE REVELATION OF RON'S OTHER LIFE

Ron didn't eagerly give Russ more information after that night. He tried to pretend it hadn't happened. The next time they worked together, Ron tried to change the subject, crack jokes, and move past it. But Russ couldn't let it go. If what Ron was saying was real, Russ's entire view of the world had shifted, and Ron wasn't talking to him about it.

So the information came in fragments. Dripped out over weeks and months, in short answers between shifts, in moments when Russ pressed hard enough that Ron would crack a little before shutting down again. What follows is the picture that formed from those fragments—Ron's claims as Russ understood them. This is Russ telling me what Ron told him, and Ron isn't talking to anyone. Ron has since ghosted Russ and any attempts to get more answers.

Since age 11, Ron claimed he'd been visiting another realm through dreams. When he fell asleep here, he woke up there—in a body that was waiting for him, a counterpart that aged and developed alongside his earthly form. Time worked differently on the other side. One night of sleep could translate to weeks or months of experience there.

> *For a thousand years in thy sight are but as yesterday when it is past, and as a watch in the night* (Psalm 90:4 KJV).

This wasn't lucid dreaming or astral projection as the New Age community describes it.

According to Ron, the place was real—geographically, physically real. He told Russ it was the basis for Tolkien's Middle-earth and Lewis's Narnia, that those authors had accessed the same realm through dreams without realizing it was an actual place. Dean Koontz, Stephen King—Ron claimed they were all pulling from the same source. "Some know it, some don't," he said. "But the stories they tell? Those aren't just from imagination."

I've heard claims like this before on the show. I've had a guest, I called Colin on Episode 646, who described remarkably similar experiences—traversing realms, spending extended time in other places during sleep. He stopped talking to me afterward, just like Ron stopped talking to Russ. That pattern alone makes me lean in rather than dismiss.

Ron's time in the other realm started as adventure—a kid waking up in a magical world. But it shifted into training. Fighting techniques that defied physics. Being given wings to fly. The ability to enter other people's dreams, plant suggestions, and gather intelligence. Ron called this "dream-walking." He rose through ranks until he became the primary enforcer for the entity called Sujent, leading operations that, according to him, affected both dimensions.

Eventually Ron met his girlfriend. He grew a conscience. He started recognizing that the things Sujent had him doing were evil. So he tried to fight back and cut ties. He thought he had destroyed Sujent, the master he once served. That's why the pulsing light terrified him so badly. He was seeing proof that his best efforts had failed.

THE BOOK THAT WASN'T FICTION

Eventually Ron got tired of Russ's questions about his dual life, and handed him a novel. "It's about me," he said. "My friend wrote it about my friends and me. It says it's fiction, but it's not fiction. We did that for deniability. Just read this and stop asking me stuff."

The author was a woman Ron had known since college, someone he described as having a natural "scribe" ability—a capacity to perceive and record supernatural events without trying. She wrote the book to document Ron and his friends' real experiences, disguising them with enough fiction to provide cover.

I've talked with this author. I learned she fled across the country to escape this story. She told me she had cast spells specifically so that Ron and anyone connected to him couldn't find her digitally. When I located her within an hour of looking—because, as she'd learn, her spells apparently didn't account for podcasters outside Ron's circle—she was stunned. We spoke for hours, across multiple conversations. She confirmed key details Russ had told me. She doesn't want to be publicly associated with any of this, and I respect that. But her existence, and her corroboration, matter.

The book, as Russ described its contents, laid out recruitment methods that followed patterns I've now heard from dozens of unrelated guests. It always started the same way:

children, in preadolescence and adolescence, having intensely vivid dreams. They described tunnel systems beneath the earth, often leading to a central chamber. And inside, entities making promises, offering them a special purpose or deal, to kids too young to understand the cost.

> ...*And he said unto me, Write: for these words are true and faithful* (Revelation 21:5 KJV).

The book also described a war between Sujent and another entity. Not metaphorical warfare—literal dimensional conflict with armies, territories, and strategic objectives that spilled into our reality. This rivalry, according to Ron, explained things I'd been trying to figure out for years: why certain locations became supernatural hotspots, why different people manifested different abilities, why the patterns of harassment varied so much between victims. If the entities weren't aligned but divided—not only opposing humanity but jockeying for power among themselves—then the chaos wasn't random at all. It was the product of a turf war.

That idea—competing factions within the fallen realm—has become one of the most important patterns *The Confessionals* has uncovered. Scripture describes a hierarchy of principalities and powers in Ephesians 6:12 and territorial spirits in Daniel 10:13. What Ron described aligns with that biblical framework in ways he probably didn't intend, because by Russ's account, Ron wasn't a believer. He was describing what he had experienced, not what he had read in the Bible. And that, to me, makes it more compelling, not less.

THE CIRCLE OF THE ENHANCED

The book about Ron's two lives also revealed things about Ron's friends that turned Russ's world upside down. When Ron was young, he had three or four of his friends try the same dream-crossing technique—and it worked. They became a crew, both in our world and the dream world. Each developed different superhuman abilities. And some of those abilities bled over into this side.

According to the book about Ron's life, Ron developed the ability to shapeshift into something monstrous—and he retained that ability, to some degree, in our world. Similarly, Ron's circle of friends could do the same. Russ revealed to me that he met a few of these friends at Ron's birthday party. As a "party trick," one of them could extend his canine teeth into fangs, right in front of everyone. Ron laughed it off, tried to play it like a joke, but Russ had already seen too many unnatural events to buy that.

"We know each other," Ron had told Russ about this network. "Not all of us, but enough. When someone new manifests abilities, word spreads. We keep track because we have to—not everyone who gets enhanced stays sane."

That last part stuck with me. I'm not suggesting that mental illness is always supernatural in origin—it isn't, and people who need medical help should receive it. But I've interviewed enough people to know that some experiences don't fit neatly into clinical categories, and the church would do well to develop better discernment about where the medical and the spiritual overlap.

THE NIGHT OF TRANSFORMATION

The next series of events, as disclosed by Russ, is where his story crosses a line that may lose some readers. I'm going to share this anyway. Russ says he saw it with his own eyes, and the details are too specific, too strange, to feel manufactured.

Separately from Ron, Russ's own brother, Derek, had been experiencing supernatural harassment from creatures watching him from outside the house, trying to get in. I have interviewed Derek, and he was able to confirm details he couldn't have known from Russ alone.

Described as monkey-like entities with huge eyes and no mouths, the creatures would appear on power lines and in trees, staring through the windows. According to what Russ would later learn, they were enforcers dispatched by the entity called Baal, sent to punish Derek for refusing to cooperate when another recruiter was attempting to claim a human child. When Derek tried to resist, the monkeys came. When he complied, they left—for a while.

One night, Russ heard scuffling and thumping above his basement bedroom. He ran upstairs and found Derek covered in scratches, panicking: "They got in. They got in. I don't know how they got in." Russ called Ron.

Ron showed up fast, pulling up in a car. They were standing outside in the cold when he told Russ, "Things are going to get really weird for a little bit. Just trust me."

And then Russ watched his friend change.

Ron closed his eyes and looked down. His legs got longer by several inches. Russ could hear what he described as creaking, like bones restructuring. In front of Russ, Ron got taller, thinner, stretched. His eyes changed. His whole personality changed.

When the transformation was complete, the thing that looked sort of like Ron but wasn't quite Ron looked at Russ and said, in a voice that was close to Ron's but yet not his normal voice: "Your friend is gone. He'll be back."

Russ stared at this transformed being, then suggested they go inside because of the cold. That's when the change Russ couldn't believe he had witnessed became undeniable. As they moved down toward the basement bedroom, "Ron" had to hunch down several inches to clear the low ledge above the stairs, something he'd never once had to do before. But the house hadn't changed. Ron had.

Once inside, the thing that wasn't quite Ron sat on the couch, hands on its knees, and stared at the wall in front of them for close to an hour. It wouldn't respond to anything Russ said. Wouldn't answer questions. Just sat there like a placeholder while Ron's consciousness, according to what Ron later explained, operated in an inverted version of their neighborhood—fighting off the monkey entities that had been stationed around the property.

> *What? Know ye not that your body is the temple of the Holy Ghost which is in you, which ye have of God, and ye are not your own?* (1 Corinthians 6:19 KJV).

What Russ describes here—a human body being temporarily vacated by its owner and occupied by another intelligence—is something Scripture has a framework for. We call it possession. The difference—and it's a critical one—is that Ron entered into this arrangement *voluntarily.* He'd made previous agreements with Sujent that gave these entities access. His counterpart from the other realm, whom he called "Scorp," served as a placeholder while Ron operated elsewhere. It was transactional. It was organized. And it was the product of years of deepening entanglement with the fallen realm.

About 40 minutes later, Ron changed back. Russ heard and saw the transformation reverse. His friend was exhausted, barely conscious. He informed Russ the problem with Derek and the monkey-like entities was "handled"—but warned him never to tell Derek what happened. If Derek knew, the awareness itself could undo the protection.

For years, it worked. The monkey entities stopped coming. Derek had no memory of what happened that night. He assumed they just went away on their own. It only unraveled again when Derek, on his own, reached back toward Baal. He reopened the door—and the entities returned.

Russ confirmed the existence of the monkey entities through his cousin, a woman with her own spiritual practices who did a viewing on Derek years later and, without any prompting, described them. "Oh, you mean the monkeys?" she said when Russ asked if Derek had ever come to her for help. She had seen them independently, becoming the third witness to the same phenomenon across different years and circumstances.

THE LOCK AND THE KEY

As the story progresses, claims made by Ron become harder to verify and even more extraordinary. Nonetheless, the experiences recounted by Russ, combined with how closely his testimony aligns with patterns I've documented across hundreds of other episodes, made it impossible to dismiss.

According to Ron, Russ existed for a specific purpose in this hidden conflict. His soul served as what Ron called a "lock"—his mere existence kept something sealed. Something that hadn't been opened since as far back as the Black Death. Ron revealed to Russ that whatever had been released during the medieval plague was the last time this particular seal had been breached, and that Russ's function was to keep it shut. Not by doing anything—just by existing. And when he died, that essence would transfer to another in his line.

Russ's brother, Derek, meanwhile, was the opposite. He was a key. An opener. His natural presence could unlock things that Baal wanted accessed. That's why Baal recruited him—not as a soldier, but as a tool. Derek didn't do anything intentionally. He would arrive wherever Baal directed him, and something would open.

A lock and a key in the same family: brothers with opposite supernatural functions. Russ himself noted the cosmic irony of it.

While I am unable to verify all of this information independently, what I can tell you is that the broader concept—that certain bloodlines carry spiritual significance, that the enemy targets specific families across generations—is thoroughly biblical. The messianic line from Abraham through David to Christ was targeted at every generation. Pharaoh tried to destroy the Hebrew firstborn. Herod tried to slaughter the children of Bethlehem. The idea that the enemy has strategic interest in specific lineages isn't Ron's invention. It's one of the oldest patterns in Scripture.

And across hundreds of episodes of *The Confessionals,* I've heard too many families describe generational supernatural experiences—parents and children encountering the same types of entities, the same patterns of harassment, the same gifts of spiritual sight—to dismiss the bloodline element as coincidence.

THE DISAPPEARANCE

The last act of Ron's story, as Russ experienced it, reads like something out of a tragedy.

Ron had tried for years to sever his connection to the entity Sujent. Despite everything—the protective measures, the deliberate isolation—the pulsing light he encountered that night with Russ proved his best efforts had failed. The bonds forged in the other realm didn't respect earthly concepts of quitting.

> *When the unclean spirit is gone out of a man, he walketh through dry places, seeking rest, and findeth none. Then he saith, I will return into my house from whence I came out…* (Matthew 12:43-44 KJV).

Ron could still project his consciousness. He had never given up using it, he said, to check in on people and situations. But that ongoing connection meant the door was never fully closed.

When I tracked down the author of Ron's book, Russ informed Ron that I had found her. Ron's response was immediate: "I'll be back." He hung up and went to check on something. When he called back, his voice sounded different.

According to Ron, when he tried to defect from Sujent, Sujent created a duplicate of him—an "evil twin" built with the same abilities but stripped of any moral conscience. Ron claimed he had managed to confine this duplicate inside what he called a "mental prison." But now, he believed it had escaped. His last words to Russ were simple: "I guess I have to try finding this thing again."

Russ has tried to make contact. Ron doesn't respond. The author also remains silent, unwilling to speak publicly. The story, from Russ's end, is frozen in place—a world-shattering revelation followed by a dial tone.

> *And no marvel; for Satan himself is transformed into an angel of light. Therefore it is no great thing if his ministers also be transformed as the ministers of righteousness…* (2 Corinthians 11:14-15 KJV).

THE PATTERN I CAN'T IGNORE

After sitting with this story for three years and chasing down every lead I could find, one conclusion keeps resurfacing.

Ron's testimony, filtered through Russ, describes an organized system: recruitment through dreams targeting children in a specific developmental window, a hierarchy of roles and specialties, competing factions among fallen entities, bloodline targeting, and a program that operates across dimensions simultaneously. These aren't things Russ had the framework to invent. He's not a theologian or a paranormal researcher. He's a seemingly ordinary guy who followed a light in the sky and had his view of the world changed forever.

But here's what haunts me. The patterns in Ron's story—the childhood recruitment, the tunnel systems, the dimensional travel, the entity rivalries, the bloodline significance—I have heard these same patterns from guests with no connection to Russ or Ron, both before and after this interview. People from different states, different decades, different walks of life, all describing the same infrastructure. The details vary, but the architecture is consistent.

That's what makes me lean into this testimony rather than dismiss it. Not that every claim is verifiable. But the patterns are. And patterns that surface independently across hundreds of unrelated witnesses aren't coincidence. They're evidence of a system.

THE WAR WITHOUT THE WARRIOR

But here's what strikes me most about Ron's story, and it's not the shapeshifting or the dimensional travel or the rival entities. It's the ending. Or rather, the lack of one.

Ron tried everything to escape Sujent. Anchors. Seals. Isolation. Countermeasures. Mental prisons. He fought with incredible skill and what seems like genuine courage. And he failed. Not because he wasn't strong enough or smart enough, but because he was using the enemy's own weapons to fight the enemy's war.

Ron, by Russ's account, was not a believer. He wasn't fighting with the authority of Jesus Christ. He was fighting with abilities gained through agreements with fallen entities, using techniques learned in their training grounds. It's like trying to escape a prison using keys the warden gave you—they'll open every door except the one that leads to actual freedom.

Compare that to what we've seen in other chapters of this book. James, running through the desert in Joshua Tree, called out the name of Jesus and felt an invisible barrier break. Hunter, floating out of his body with a gray entity in his yard, said "Jesus" and was slammed back into his body instantly. Every time the name of Christ was invoked with genuine faith, the entities responded immediately. Every time someone tried to fight on their own terms, the battle dragged on without resolution.

> *And they were all amazed, and spake among themselves, saying, What a word is this! for with authority and power he commandeth the unclean spirits, and they come out* (Luke 4:36 KJV).

Ron's story is, in many ways, the most compelling argument in this entire book for why Jesus Christ isn't optional in spiritual warfare. He's essential. Not as a philosophy. Not as a cultural tradition. As Lord. Because when you're dealing with principalities and powers that can bend perception, manipulate memory, and speak languages given by fallen angels, you need more than human strength. You need divine authority.

Ron had power. What he didn't have was authority. There's a difference. Power is what the enemy gives you to keep you in the game. Authority is what Christ gives you to end it.

> ...*greater is he that is in you, than he that is in the world* (1 John 4:4 KJV).

THE DARK SHIFT CONTINUES

Somewhere tonight, a child around the age of 11 is going to fall asleep and dream of a tunnel that leads to a chamber where something is waiting with an offer. Somewhere, a person who made agreements with entities years ago is trying to break free and discovering that the chains don't unlock from the inside. Somewhere, a set of brothers exists with opposite purposes in a conflict they didn't choose and barely understand.

These stories aren't unique. They represent a pattern I've documented across years of interviews—a vast, hidden theater of operations where human and non-human agents interact across dimensional boundaries in ways our churches barely acknowledge and our culture actively mocks.

Ron's story ended in silence and uncertainty. It doesn't have to end that way for you. If these testimonies have stirred something in you—fear, recognition, or even just a nagging sense that the world is stranger and more dangerous than you've been told—then the question isn't whether this is real. The question is what you're going to do about it.

The entities are organized. The recruitment never stops. The veil is thinner than we imagined. But the One who created all dimensions still holds authority over every realm, and the name of Jesus still makes every knee bow—in Heaven, on earth, and in the places between.

> *Finally, my brethren, be strong in the Lord, and in the power of his might. Put on the whole armour of God, that ye may be able to stand against the wiles of the devil* (Ephesians 6:10-11 KJV).

Ron's interdimensional ordeals, James's escape from the desert portal, Hunter's prophetic visions, Kyle's battle in the Daniel Boone, Charlie's encounter with the Enochian craft—all of these stories, different as they are on the surface, share the same architecture underneath. The same childhood recruitment windows. The same dimensional crossings. The same hierarchy of fallen powers is competing with each other while serving the same ultimate agenda: the eternal separation of humanity from God.

The threads are all here. It's time to pull them together.

But before I do, sit with this: Ron had every ability the enemy could give him, and it wasn't enough to set him free. That tells you everything you need to know about whose side you want to be on.

12
The Convergence

Now the Spirit speaketh expressly, that in the latter times some shall depart from the faith, giving heed to seducing spirits, and doctrines of devils.

—1 Timothy 4:1 KJV

Every story in this book is about the same war.

I know they don't look the same on the surface. A trucker in Pennsylvania sees lights in the sky. A 15-year-old boy in Kentucky fights for his life against a creature that walks on two legs. A soldier finds a language that shouldn't exist on a craft that shouldn't be here. A man in Indiana watches his friend's body stretch and change in his driveway while something else takes control.

A worship pastor in Tennessee wakes up with claw marks from a dream. A kid from Joshua Tree barely escapes a ritual designed to tear open a portal between dimensions. A podcaster gets tricked by a satanist and carries the spiritual weight for years.

Different faces. Different locations. Different decades. But the same war.

After hundreds of episodes of *The Confessionals,* after sitting across from people whose stories would make most churches uncomfortable and most skeptics furious, I've stopped seeing these as separate categories. Cryptids. UFOs. Demons. Interdimensional entities. Shadow people. Those categories exist because we need language to talk about the impossible. But the more I listen, the more I'm convinced that the boxes themselves are part of the deception. They keep us arguing about what something is instead of asking the more important question: who is behind it, and what do they want?

> *And no marvel; for Satan himself is transformed into an angel of light* (2 Corinthians 11:14 KJV).

The same entities that wrote Enochian on the screen of Charlie's downed craft are the same entities that recruit children through dreams the way Ron was recruited at 11 years old. The same principalities that sent a dogman to terrorize Kyle in the Daniel Boone National Forest are the same powers that orchestrated the sonic portal in Joshua Tree. The same fallen beings that dispatched human agents to follow me into my home are the same forces that gifted forbidden knowledge to humanity before the flood.

They wear whatever mask serves the moment. Show a soldier something technological. Show a hunter something bestial. Show a child something magical. Show a spiritual seeker something "enlightening." The costume changes, but the fingerprint is always the same: entities operating from the second heaven, working through a hierarchy of competing factions that still serve the same ultimate agenda—the eternal separation of humanity from God.

That's the pattern. And I'm not the only one who sees it.

THE MEN BEHIND THE CURTAIN

As I write this, I'm gearing up for a meeting that I never expected to be part of.

It started at a conference, the way a lot of things in my life have started—a conversation that felt casual but wasn't. I met a man, and as we talked, it became clear that he was operating at a level of this conversation that I had only glimpsed from the outside. He wasn't a podcaster or a researcher. He was the real deal—former special operations, deeply committed to Christ, and embedded in a network of men who had spent years doing something most people would never believe.

These men are former special operations soldiers. Christians. Their mission is to infiltrate the groups and individuals driving what the world calls "disclosure"—the government's slow-drip revelation that unidentified aerial phenomena are real—and uncover what is actually happening behind the scenes. They've spent years inside this world, and what they've found confirms everything I've been hearing from my guests, but with a clarity and specificity that comes from operating at the intelligence level.

We communicated extensively through text and phone calls. The organization's leaders debriefed me on what they had discovered, and they didn't mince words. What follows is what they shared with me, and I'll tell you upfront: this isn't speculation from fringe researchers. This is intelligence gathered by trained operators who understand how deception campaigns work because they've run them for a living.

Here's what they told me.

The technology behind UAPs—what people are calling UFOs—is fallen-angel technology. It's not extraterrestrial in the way the world wants to believe. It's interdimensional, and it's being gifted to humanity for reverse engineering. When we hear that a craft was "shot down" or "recovered," they said it was allowed to be shot down. Sometimes it doesn't even require shooting. The craft is delivered. Intentionally.

> *And the angels which kept not their first estate, but left their own habitation, he hath reserved in everlasting chains under darkness unto the judgment of the great day* (Jude 1:6 KJV).

The gifting is the part that should make every Bible-reading Christian sit up straight. Because we've seen this before. The book of Enoch describes the watchers—fallen angels—teaching humanity things we were never meant to know. Metalworking for weapons. Sorcery. Enchantments. Cosmetics used for seduction. Knowledge that corrupted humanity so thoroughly that God had to flood the earth to reset the board.

New day, old tricks.

The more humanity reverse-engineers this forbidden technology, the further the divide grows between God and us. Because as we accelerate toward capabilities we were never designed to have, we start feeling more and more like gods ourselves. Which is, of course, the original play. The serpent in the Garden didn't offer Eve technology. He offered her something more dangerous: *"Ye shall be as gods, knowing good and evil"* (Genesis 3:5 KJV). The technology is just the vehicle. The destination is the same as it's always been—human pride replacing divine authority.

The operators also shared with me something critical about the disclosure community itself. There are a lot of bad actors in it, and they all have their own agendas. They're not all on the same page. Levels of involvement vary. Some are true other-worldly believers who genuinely think they're helping humanity. Some are in it for the money or the fame. And some know exactly what they're doing and who they're serving. These guys aren't all on the same team, and not all of the interests at play are human.

WHAT'S COMING

Nobody knows exactly what disclosure is going to look like. But I have a pretty good idea of where it's headed, and what these men shared with me lines up with patterns I've been documenting for years.

At some point, world leaders are going to tell the entire planet that we are not alone in the universe. They will likely provide craft, biological materials, and possibly bodies. Physical evidence. Tangible, examinable, undeniable evidence. And the phrase that will underpin everything is the one that has always been the enemy's favorite weapon: "Seeing is believing."

Most people won't understand that metallic physical objects and craft can be—and are—created in other realms and brought here supernaturally. We've been trained to think that if you can touch it, weigh it, and run tests on it, then it must be what it appears to be. But that's the trick. The enemy has spent generations convincing us that the physical world is all there is, and now he's going to use physical evidence to sell us the biggest lie in human history.

When biological bodies are presented—and they will be, whether we're talking about bodies recovered from craft or produced through programs that have been running for decades—many people will be swept away. One narrative that may emerge is that these beings are humans from the future, or an advanced branch of human evolution, here to help us ascend to the next level of consciousness. Their DNA may show at least some human ancestry, and that will be treated as proof. But it won't be proof of what they claim.

There is a hybrid program at work. These entities abduct people and harvest DNA. What the world will call evidence of alien biology may actually be evidence of a breeding program conducted by the fallen—engineered bodies presenting half-truths dressed up as revelation.

And if you think that kind of program sounds too far-fetched for our world, consider what we already know was happening in plain sight.

Jeffrey Epstein wasn't just running a trafficking operation. The trafficking was the motor, but it wasn't the machine. It was the foundation on which he built something far darker. Epstein was funding cutting-edge genetic research—pouring tens of millions of dollars into elite scientists working on CRISPR gene editing, re-genesis technology, and the belief that organisms could be engineered from scratch. The trafficking of children provided the raw material. The science provided the methodology. And the endgame wasn't just exploitation—it was the manipulation of human DNA itself.

I've sat across from survivors of Epstein's network on my show, and what they've told me goes far beyond the massage parlor narrative that mainstream media was comfortable reporting. One survivor described being subjected to DNA mixing from childhood—treated like a petri dish, called a "mixed breed" by her handlers because they had deliberately combined different bloodlines in her genetic makeup.

They engineered children to physically resemble their assigned handlers so no one would question the family structure in public. Another survivor detailed how the trafficking wasn't the point—it was the tool that funded and concealed the real operation: genetic experimentation, ritual abuse, and programs designed to blur the line between what's human and what isn't.

Does that sound familiar? It should. Because it's exactly what the watchers did before the flood. They took human women, corrupted human DNA, produced hybrid offspring, and taught humanity forbidden knowledge. The book of Enoch says these actions so defiled the earth that God had to destroy it with water and start over.

And here we are, thousands of years later, watching the same program run through modern institutions, modern science, and modern money. Epstein is gone, but the infrastructure he helped build is still operational. The survivors I've spoken to are clear on this point: he was a middleman, not the architect. The machine didn't stop when he died. It just swapped out one wheel for another.

So when disclosure presents biological bodies with partially human DNA and the world gasps at the "proof" of alien life, remember what you now know. There are programs on this earth—funded by billionaires, protected by intelligence agencies, built on the blood of children—that have been engineering hybrid biology for decades. The bodies they show us don't have to come from another planet. They just have to look like they did.

> *For there shall arise false Christs, and false prophets, and shall shew great signs and wonders; insomuch that, if it were possible, they shall deceive the very elect* (Matthew 24:24 KJV).

Here's what you need to understand about the spiritual setup. We are humans, yes, but we are very much spiritual beings. And for generations, we've been raised in a culture that told us there is no God, that we evolved from nothing, that the material world is all there is. That didn't happen by accident. It created a spiritual vacuum. It starved entire generations of the one thing every human soul was designed to hunger for—connection to their Creator.

We have reached a point where humanity is starving for a spiritual existence. The hunger pains are so intense that when someone finally offers food, most people won't stop to ask what's in it. They'll just eat. Think of it this way: a starving child standing on a street with a candy store on one side and a steakhouse on the other. The child doesn't have the patience or the understanding to wait for a real meal to be prepared. The candy is right there. It's sweet. It's immediate. It fills the emptiness for a moment. But it doesn't nourish. It doesn't sustain. And too much of it will kill you.

Christianity is the steakhouse. It takes time. You work out your salvation with fear and trembling, as Paul wrote in Philippians 2:12. You grow in understanding and wisdom over years of relationship with Christ. It's not flashy. It doesn't promise instant enlightenment or cosmic consciousness. It promises something better—truth, freedom, and eternal life through the only One who has authority over every dimension, every principality, and every power.

The new-age religion that will emerge from disclosure—and make no mistake, a new world religion is the endgame—will be the candy store. Quick-hit spirituality. Instant connection to "higher beings." The promise of ascension without repentance, enlightenment without surrender, cosmic citizenship without the Cross. It will taste incredible on the surface, and it will destroy everyone who swallows it.

THE SLOW BURN

I'm already seeing it happen, and that's what terrifies me most. Not the dramatic disclosure event that's coming—that will be catastrophic, yes, but at least it will be obvious. What terrifies me is what's happening right now, in the quiet spaces where Christians think they're safe.

People who love Jesus are coming across information online—videos, podcasts, articles about UAPs, consciousness, ancient aliens, simulation theory, remote viewing—and it's planting seeds of doubt they don't even recognize. They don't wake up one morning and decide to abandon their faith. It's slower than that. They start making small exceptions in their theology.

They start thinking, *Well, maybe Genesis doesn't mean exactly what it says.* They start entertaining ideas that feel intellectually sophisticated but are actually ancient heresies with modern packaging.

Little by little, they drift toward a fence—the dividing line between biblical truth and the broader "spiritual but not religious" worldview that our culture celebrates. They become fence-sitters in their faith. One foot in Christ, one foot in curiosity about things the Bible explicitly warns against. And they don't realize how dangerous that position is until the wind hits.

> *I know thy works, that thou art neither cold nor hot: I would thou wert cold or hot. So then because thou art lukewarm, and neither cold nor hot, I will spue thee out of my mouth* (Revelation 3:15-16 KJV).

Those fence-sitters will be the first to flip when hard disclosure comes. When the bodies are displayed, and the craft are demonstrated, and the beings present themselves as our benefactors, the people who never fully committed to Christ will fall away faster than we've ever seen. But it won't stop there.

Disclosure will be so explosive, so paradigm-shattering, that people who thought their faith was strong will discover it was built on cultural Christianity rather than genuine relationship with Jesus. They'll drop like flies. Not because the evidence is compelling—though it will be designed to look overwhelming—but because their foundation was never deep enough to withstand the storm.

Jesus told the parable for exactly this moment:

> *And every one that heareth these sayings of mine, and doeth them not, shall be likened unto a foolish man, which built his house upon the sand: And the rain descended, and the floods came, and the winds blew, and beat upon that house; and it fell: and great was the fall of it* (Matthew 7:26-27 KJV).

The rain is coming. The question isn't whether your house will be tested. The question is what it's built on.

THE MISSION AHEAD

The meeting I'm heading to this weekend isn't about gathering more evidence. I have plenty of evidence. Nearly a decade of *The Confessionals* has given me more evidence than most people could process in a lifetime. This meeting is about something more urgent: equipping the Church before the wave hits.

The men I'm meeting with—intelligence backgrounds, political connections, former operators who've seen things that would break most people—they have one goal. They want to educate pastors. They want to debrief Christian leaders on what is happening behind the scenes of disclosure so that when it goes public, pastors are equipped to lead their congregations biblically instead of scrambling for answers or, worse, dismissing the whole thing and losing their people in the process.

That's the real danger for the Church. Not that pastors will fall for the deception, but that they'll pretend it's not happening. They'll treat disclosure the same way the Western Church has treated the supernatural for the past century—as something too weird, too uncomfortable, too far outside what they learned in seminary to touch. And while they bury their heads, their people will go looking for answers somewhere else. And the answers they find will lead them straight into the arms of the very entities this book has been warning about.

I wrote in Chapter 1 that the Western Church has done a really good job of stripping the supernatural out of the Bible and our sermons. That sentence feels almost quaint to me now.

Stripping the supernatural out of Church didn't just leave a gap in our theology; it left our people defenseless against a deception that is supernatural to its core. You can't fight what you refuse to acknowledge exists.

> *My people are destroyed for lack of knowledge: because thou hast rejected knowledge, I will also reject thee…* (Hosea 4:6 KJV).

The stories in this book aren't just strange tales from the fringes. They're intelligence reports from the front lines of a war that most churches pretend isn't happening. Charlie's Enochian craft shows us the enemy's technology. Ron's recruitment shows us their methods. Kyle's dogman shows us their manifestations. James's desert portal shows us their human infrastructure. Hunter's prophecy shows us that God is still warning His people, still pulling back the veil, still sending messages through imperfect vessels to prepare us for what's ahead.

Every testimony in this book points to the same conclusion. And I've been circling it for 12 chapters because I wanted you to see the evidence before I stated it plainly.

Here it is.

If this is real—if the supernatural realm is this active, this organized, this specifically hostile toward humanity—then there is only one reasonable response.

And that response has a name.

13

The Only Reasonable Response

Jesus saith unto him, I am the way, the truth, and the life: no man cometh unto the Father, but by me.

—John 14:6 KJV

I need to take you back to the beginning before I take you to the end.

I was a trailer-park kid in Kutztown, Pennsylvania, who saw lights in the sky and felt something watching him in the woods. I was the grandson of a man who laid hands on the sick and watched them walk away healed—a man whose bloodline I didn't share but whose mantle would one day fall to me. I was the young man who lost his grandfather and discovered that his faith had been borrowed, not owned. I was the young husband who nearly destroyed his marriage because he was building on a foundation that didn't exist.

I was the man sitting in a red brick church at a funeral I didn't want to attend, hearing the gospel for the hundredth time, when suddenly the Holy Spirit cut through everything and said, "You don't need to change to come to Me. Just come to Me, and I'll change you."

I was the trucker on Germantown Pike who heard God say he was going to start a podcast and work with a man named Wes Germer from *Sasquatch Chronicles*—and didn't want any of it. I was the new believer who walked into a satanist's house carrying a Bible and naive confidence, and walked out carrying a spiritual weight that would muffle the voice of God for years. I was the podcaster who sat behind a microphone week after week, listening to people confess the impossible, slowly realizing that every story was a different window into the same war.

And now I'm the man who has to tell you what all of it means.

WHEN THE WAR CAME HOME

In April 2025, I was on set filming a television show called *The Counter* with my friends Troy Brewer, Joseph Z, Alan DiDio, Darren Stott, and Bryan Schwartz. During a break, I asked them to pray with me for my wife, Lindsay. She was going through testing for possible breast cancer.

I asked for that prayer the way you'd ask someone to pass the salt. A routine checklist thing. I didn't believe my 39-year-old wife had breast cancer. Not really. She was young, healthy, and attentive to her body. The testing was just a precaution. The prayer was just a formality.

The following week, I was minutes away from recording an interview when my phone rang. Lindsay was on the other end, sobbing. She was apologizing to me, and I was confused because my wife is one of the most careful, intentional people I've ever known. I couldn't imagine what she had done that warranted this level of anguish.

Then she said, "I have cancer."

My world stopped. Everything went muffled. I don't remember hanging up. I don't remember walking to my car. I remember driving, and I remember calling my pastor out of desperation and despair, and I remember that what followed over the next two weeks was confusion, impossible decision-making, and guttural sobbing. The kind that comes from a place I didn't know existed inside me.

Through prayer, Lindsay and I came to understand that this was a spiritual battle as much as a physical one. That conviction became absolute when, the same week Lindsay was diagnosed, my father had a heart attack and was hospitalized.

I need you to understand the timing.

God was broadening the path He had us on. I was connecting with pastors across the country who saw the value of my podcasting ministry. I had just accepted the call to preach—the same evangelistic calling I'd run from since Bible college. I was scheduled to deliver my second sermon ever, the Sunday of the week Lindsay was diagnosed.

The enemy seemed okay with me interviewing people about their experiences from behind a microphone, one broadcast a week. But the moment I stepped out from behind the screen and into the pulpit—the moment I started taking all the intelligence I'd gathered over nearly a decade and using it offensively, preaching the gospel as an evangelist to see people come to Christ—the warfare kicked up to levels we had never experienced.

> *Yea, and all that will live godly in Christ Jesus shall suffer persecution* (2 Timothy 3:12 KJV).

My pastor told me I didn't have to preach that Sunday. He said nobody would blame me if it was too much.

I preached anyway.

I stood behind that pulpit and told my church what had happened. Then I preached a sermon that my pastor later said sounded like I'd been doing it for years. That wasn't me. That was the Holy Spirit's fire flowing through a broken vessel. Because I was broken. But broken doesn't mean defeated. Broken means you finally stop relying on yourself and let God work through the cracks.

I told my church something that day, and I'm going to tell you now.

I was already planning on kicking in the enemy's teeth for the rest of my life. But now he woke up a sleeping giant. Now it won't just be me—it will be my wife, my Spear-Bearer, who will make their existence hell, until the Lord returns or He takes us home. I am not about to back down. I will double down.

As I write this, Lindsay and I are still overcoming her cancer. The battle is ongoing. But the diagnosis changed me. It took me from a man who was trying to be gentle about what he knew, to a man with a sense of urgency. Gentleness got me nowhere. I see the enemy's battle plans now, and I will spend the rest of my life exposing them.

We are in a spiritual war, and it's time to stop pretending otherwise.

THE LOGICAL CASE

Let me lay this out the way I would if you were sitting across from me in my studio.

If even one of the testimonies in this book is true—just one—then the implications are staggering. If Charlie found Enochian text on a craft that wasn't made by humans, then non-human intelligences are real, and they're using the language of fallen angels. If Kyle's dogman stood up on two legs and hunted him through the forest, then entities from another realm can take physical form. If Hunter dreamed about my house with 98 percent accuracy and saw cloaked figures following me inside, then prophetic sight is real and human agents serve dark masters. If James watched people levitate through a green portal in Joshua Tree, then organized groups can tear open dimensional barriers using ritualized frequency. If Ron's body transformed in Russ's driveway while another intelligence occupied it, then human beings can be vessels for interdimensional exchange.

If any of this is true—and I believe all of it is, because I've spent years verifying what I can and watching the patterns converge across hundreds of unrelated witnesses—then we are not living in the world we were told we're living in. We are living in a supernatural war zone where organized fallen intelligences actively work to deceive, recruit, and ultimately destroy human beings.

And if that's the reality we're in, then you need to ask yourself a very simple question: *What protection do I have?*

Not what theory. Not what philosophy. Not what spiritual practice makes you feel centered. What actual, tested, verified protection do you have against entities that can bend perception, cross dimensions, speak ancient languages, and manipulate human biology?

Because every testimony in this book answers that question the same way.

James ran through the desert calling on the name of Jesus, and an invisible barrier broke. Hunter said "Jesus" while floating out of his body, and was slammed back into himself instantly. My grandfather spoke the blood of Jesus over a demonized woman, and something inside her screamed and fled. Rob laid hands on me and prayed in the authority of Christ, and a spiritual weight I had carried for years lifted in seconds. In the overwhelming majority of cases I've documented, the name of Jesus Christ produced immediate results against entities that no human power could touch.

And in every case where someone tried to fight without Christ—Ron with his interdimensional abilities, Derek with his occult connections, the partygoers at Joshua Tree with their rituals and frequencies—the battle either continued without resolution or the person sank deeper into bondage.

> *Neither is there salvation in any other: for there is none other name under heaven given among men, whereby we must be saved* (Acts 4:12 KJV).

This isn't a religious opinion. It's an observation from the data. Across hundreds of interviews, across every type of supernatural encounter I've documented, the name of Jesus Christ is the most consistently effective intervention that exists. Nothing else comes close. I'll be honest—I've heard a small number of testimonies where someone invoked the name, and the experience didn't immediately stop. I'm still wrestling with those cases.

But I think Scripture gives us the framework: Jesus told His disciples that certain entities only respond to prayer and fasting (Matthew 17:21), and the sons of Sceva learned the hard way in Acts 19 that the name of Jesus isn't a magic word—it carries authority proportional to your genuine relationship with Christ. The name works because of whose name it is. But it's not an incantation. It's an appeal to the living King, and the depth of your connection to that King matters.

What I can tell you without hesitation is this: across nearly a decade of documentation, the name of Jesus is the only intervention that works at all. Every other method—occult rituals, meditation, mental resistance, ignoring it, fighting back physically—either fails outright or drags the person deeper in. Jesus is the only name that makes these things respond. And in the vast majority of cases, that response is immediate and total.

If you're reading this and you consider yourself a rational person, then follow the evidence to its conclusion. Accepting Jesus Christ as your personal Lord and Savior isn't one option among many. It's the only reasonable response to reality.

THE INVITATION

I want to talk to three groups of people right now.

If you picked up this book because you're fascinated by the paranormal—by UFOs, cryptids, ghosts, the unexplained—I want you to hear me clearly. What you're fascinated by is real. But it's not what the world tells you it is.

These aren't visitors from another planet here to help us evolve. These aren't spirits of the dead lingering between worlds. These aren't undiscovered species hiding in our forests. These are fallen beings—angels who rebelled against God, entities operating from the second heaven, principalities and powers that have been at war with humanity since Eden. They wear every mask. They tell every lie. And they have one goal: to keep you separated from the only One who can save you.

If the supernatural is real enough to fascinate you, then God is real enough to save you. Don't let curiosity lead you into the arms of the very things you should be running from.

If you're a Christian who has been sleepwalking through your faith—going to church on Sundays but never really engaging with Scripture, never building a genuine prayer life, never confronting the reality that you're in a war—I need you to wake up. Right now. Not next month. Not when things get scary. Now. Because by the time disclosure hits, it will be too late to start building your foundation.

The storm doesn't wait for you to pour concrete. What's coming will shake everything that can be shaken, and if your faith is built on tradition, comfort, or cultural Christianity rather than a personal, living relationship with Jesus Christ, you will be swept away. Get rooted in the Word. Get connected to a Bible-teaching church body that will support you when the confusion hits.

Stop being a fence-sitter. Pick a side and stand on it.

And if you're a pastor reading this—I know it's unlikely, but I'm praying you are—your people need you to stop ignoring the supernatural. They're already encountering it. They're watching videos about UAPs and ancient aliens and consciousness exploration, and they're coming to you with questions you don't have answers for, or worse, they're not coming to you at all because they assume you will dismiss them. When disclosure goes mainstream, your congregation is going to look to you for guidance. If all you can offer is silence or dismissal, they will find someone else to guide them. And the guides waiting in the wings don't serve your God. Pay attention. Your flock's eternity may depend on it.

THE STEP

If you've read this book and something inside you is saying, "This is real, and I'm not protected," then I want to give you the simplest, most important step you'll ever take.

And I'm not saying this from some high horse. I'm saying it as a man who almost lost everything because he didn't have a real foundation. I told you in Chapter 3 about the hollow frame—how I borrowed my grandfather's faith instead of building my own, how I nearly destroyed my marriage because I was standing on nothing, how I sat on that couch one morning and just stopped opening my Bible because I couldn't hear God anymore.

I know what it feels like to be exposed. I know what it feels like to realize the storm is coming and you have nothing underneath you. If I'm asking you to get right with God, it's because I've been the guy who wasn't right, and I've seen where that road ends.

It doesn't require a church building, a priest, or a ceremony. It doesn't require you to clean up your life first. God told me that unexpectedly at a church funeral I didn't want to go to: "You don't need to change to come to Me. Just come to Me, and I'll change you." It doesn't require understanding everything in this book or having all your questions answered. It just requires honesty.

Tell God you're a sinner. Everyone is. That's not an insult; it's the starting line. Tell Him you believe His Son Jesus Christ died on the Cross for your sins and rose from the dead three days later. Tell Him you want Jesus to be the Lord of your life—not just a concept you agree with, but the authority you submit to. Ask Him to forgive you. Ask Him to fill you with His Holy Spirit. Mean it.

That's it. That's the prayer of repentance. Those are the most powerful words a human being can speak, because it activates the only Authority in the universe that makes every principality, every power, every ruler of darkness, and every wicked thing in high places bow.

> *That if thou shalt confess with thy mouth the Lord Jesus, and shalt believe in thine heart that God hath raised him from the dead, thou shalt be saved* (Romans 10:9 KJV).

After you pray that prayer, do three things.

First, find a local Bible-teaching church and get involved. Not a building where you sit in the back and check a box. A body of believers who will walk with you, pray with you, challenge you, and hold you up when the storms come. You need community. The enemy isolates. God gathers.

Second, start reading the book of John. It's the fourth book in the New Testament, and it will introduce you to who Jesus Christ actually is—not the watered-down, culturally safe Jesus the world is comfortable with, but the Son of God who spoke the universe into existence, who cast out demons with a word, who walked out of His own tomb, and who is coming back.

Third, pray. Every day. Not elaborate prayers. Just talk to Him. Tell Him what scares you. Tell Him what you don't understand. Ask Him to teach you His voice the way He taught me—slowly, patiently, the way a parent teaches a newborn their language. The more time you spend with Him, the more you will recognize when He speaks. And in the days ahead, you're going to need to hear Him clearly.

THE GUARDIAN'S WATCH

As mentioned previously, my name means "Guardian of the Frontier." My wife's maiden name means "Spear-Bearer." I didn't discover that until I was nearly 40 years old, but God knew it before either of us was born.

I've spent my life standing at the edge of the veil, listening to what comes through, documenting what people see, and trying to make sense of a world that is far more supernatural than we were ever taught. *The Confessionals* has given me a front-row seat to the invisible war that surrounds every human being on the planet. And everything I've seen, everything I've heard, everything I've endured—from the lights over that Pennsylvania trailer park, to the weight that was lifted off me at Alan DiDio's conference, to the day my wife called me sobbing with a diagnosis that was meant to take me out of the fight—all of it has led me to one unshakable conviction:

> *Jesus Christ is real. The war is real. The enemy is organized, ancient, intelligent, and active. And the time to choose your side is right now.*

I think about my grandfather's campground sometimes. Those cars rolling up to the gate in the Pennsylvania darkness, filled with men who came to destroy something they didn't understand. And the angels standing shoulder to shoulder across the entrance, a wall of fire between the darkness and God's people.

The men in those cars couldn't get past the line. Not one of them even tried. They saw the angels, and they turned around and went home. That's the power of God. Not our power. Not our cleverness. Not our technology or our special operations or our podcasting platforms. God's power.

That same God is stationing His army around His people right now. The disclosure is coming. The deception is being prepared. The entities behind it have been rehearsing this moment for millennia. But they've already lost. They lost at the Cross. They lost at the empty tomb. And they know it. Revelation 12:12 (KJV) says the devil has come down with great wrath *"...because he knoweth that he hath but a short time."*

His time is short. But yours doesn't have to be.

If these accounts are true—if the supernatural realm is this active and organized against humanity—then accepting Jesus Christ as your personal Savior isn't just one option among many.

It's the only reasonable response to reality.

> *He which testifieth these things saith, Surely I come quickly. Amen. Even so, come, Lord Jesus* (Revelation 22:20 KJV).

About Tony Merkel

Tony Merkel is the creator of *The Confessionals* where the unexplained meets raw, firsthand testimony. Through in-depth conversations, we explore encounters with the supernatural, interdimensional phenomena, cryptids, and mysteries that defy conventional understanding. From eerie paranormal activity and chilling dogman sightings to UFOs, UAPs, and government cover-ups, each episode pulls back the veil on the hidden forces shaping our reality. If you're drawn to the unknown, step into *The Confessionals,* where the stories are real and the mysteries are endless.

As a creator, Tony often has ideas and topics he wants to explore that don't quite align with the branding of his main channel, @theconfessionalspodcast. That's where his YouTube channel comes in. Here, you'll find a mix of personalized content, reaction videos, deep thoughts, and even sermons he has preached.

Contact Information
https://www.theconfessionalspodcast.com
https://www.youtube.com/channel/UCumRoq4stXAAVsSo5Js1_sg

In the Right Hands, This Book Will Change Lives!

Most of the people who need this message will not be looking for this book. To change their lives, you need to **put a copy of this book in their hands.**

Our ministry is constantly seeking methods to find the people who need this anointed message to change their lives. **Will you help us reach these people?**

Extend this ministry by sowing three, five, ten, or *even more* books today and change people's lives for the better! Your generosity will be part of catalyzing the Great Awakening that many have been prophesying and praying for.